BONES
The Mystery of
Plympton Cottage

Also by Time is an Ocean
The Adventures of Nathan Sunnybank
The Hill - Songs and Poems of Darkness and Light
Another Hill – Songs and Poems of Love and Theft
Asian Voices
Asian Voices – the Director's Cut
Blood in the Cracks
Don't Look Down
Luminance - Words for a World Gone Wrong
Death in Grimsby

About the author
Nic Outterside was an award-winning newspaper journalist
and editor for 28 years and currently is the proprietor of
Time is an Ocean, the book publishing arm of **write***ahead*.
Bones is his ninth paperback book.

BONES
The Mystery of Plympton Cottage

Nic Outterside

Time is an Ocean Publications

Time is an Ocean Publications
An Imprint of **write***ahead*
Lonsdale Road
Wolverhampton, WV3 0DY

DEDICATION

For Gill, Nathan, Clare, my mother,
Whitchurch friends and the spirits of
Plympton Cottage, wherever they walk,
who all helped make this book a reality.

CONTENTS

Foreword

The truth lies within us all. Just because you may not believe something does not mean it isn't true.

Truth, like knowledge, is surprisingly difficult to define. We seem to rely on it almost every moment of every day and it's very close to each of us. Yet it is hard to define because as soon as you think you have it pinned down, some case or counter example immediately shows deficiencies in what you previously thought was true. Ironically, every definition of truth that philosophers over many centuries have developed falls prey to the question: *"But is it really true?"*

Put simply, we can only define truth as a statement about the way we believe the world actually is.

And for me this story is just that: this is the way I believe the world actually is.

The book you are holding is a fully researched narrative account which covers 18 months of my life when everything I once believed to be sacred and true was overturned spiritually, metaphysically and academically. The world I had lived in all my life suddenly became a mystery and a riddle, and the universe I thought I understood showed itself to be way beyond my imagination.

So before I begin the tale, I ask one simple question: do you believe in ghosts?

According to recent research, six out of 10 people in the UK DO believe in ghosts and 23 per cent of us think there are, or have been, unexplained or paranormal occurrences in our own homes.

And before you dismiss what I have just written, I must inform you that everything within the pages of this book is a true and detailed factual account of what happened to me and my family between June 2013 and January 2015.

John Cale once wrote: *"Fear is a man's best friend."*

No matter how brave you might think you are, fear is always just around the corner.

1

Natural human fear of the unexplained plays on our phobic pressure points. These are fears based on our individual phobias, like the fear of spiders, or rats, regular patterns, darkness, fire, heights or even water.

These can all be rationalised and the fears unlocked. But the fear of the unexplained or paranormal has a clear limit when it traverses what we can explain rationally or prove scientifically.

The grandfather of modern supernatural fiction is American author HP Lovecraft and his works draw together our ever-expanding universe, our unconscious mind, the unexplained, and what we might call ghosts.

In one of his early tales, **Beyond the Wall of Sleep**, first published in 1919, Lovecraft made some telling observations:

"I have often wondered if the majority of mankind ever pause to reflect upon the occasionally titanic significance of dreams, and of the obscure world to which they belong.

Whilst the greater number of our nocturnal visions are perhaps no more than faint and fantastic reflections of our waking experiences, there are still a certain remainder whose unmundane and ethereal character permit no ordinary interpretation, and whose vaguely exciting and disquieting effect suggests possible minute glimpses into a sphere of mental existence no less important than physical life, yet separated from that life by an all but impassable barrier.

From my experience I cannot doubt but that man, when lost to terrestrial consciousness, is indeed sojourning in another and incorporeal life of a far different nature from the life we know, and of which only the slightest and most indistinct memories linger after waking.

From those blurred and fragmentary memories we may infer much, yet prove little. We may guess that in dreams life, matter, and vitality, as the earth knows such things, are not necessarily constant; and that time and space do not exist as our waking selves comprehend them.

Sometimes I believe that this less material life is our truer life, and that our vain presence on the terraqueous globe is itself the secondary or merely virtual phenomenon."

Bones – the Mystery of Plympton Cottage is a true tale of the paranormal, the human consciousness, dreams incorporeal, the living and the dead, and our understanding of what is real and true.

This book is a personal voyage of trying to understand something both incredible and beyond most imaginations. It is also a type of mystery play which will leave you with more questions than answers.

As you read this book, you may need to pinch yourself, read things twice over, return to earlier passages to remake some connections, blur some edges of your understanding and breathe… but don't blink!

Nic Outterside
30 September 2019

Chapter One
Genesis

"Be hole, be dust, be dream, be wind, be night, be dark, be wish, be mind, Now slip, now slide, now move unseen, above, beneath, betwixt, between."
Neil Gaiman

Before I begin, let me set out a few facts before the lines get blurred. And I promise you the lines between pinching reality and the unexplained will get blurred more than once.

I am a rational and logical thinker, and until recently a true sceptic… but that has now changed forever. Now I know there is something paranormal in our world which we do not yet understand and which at the time of writing this book I cannot begin to explain.

I am also a history graduate, a former history teacher and a research scholar; the reason for me mentioning these facts will become evident as you read further.

Let me put all this into some perspective for you, and tell the story exactly as it happened.

My late father Ray was an atheist, an aircraft designer (he even designed part of Concorde) and above all a cynic. He also had an enquiring mind and taught me from an early age to only believe what I can see with my own eyes, prove scientifically and rationalise with logic.

He has sadly been dead more than 10 years now, and how I wish he had been alive to witness what I am about to tell.

But his legacy is still living in the values he instilled in me.

As for me, now in my sixties, I am a Deist and an evolutionist. I believe in the existence of a God, but not a religious or spiritual pathway to find him/her/it. And until 2013 I did not believe in any so-called hereafter nor did I believe in ghosts or spirits.

After all, I had been a multi award-winning investigative newspaper journalist for more than 28 years and by the very nature of my work had to deal in hard proven facts. If any of those facts turned out to be fictional or could not be proven with absolute veritas, then I would find myself in very hot water or even be sued in court. Thankfully that never happened.

But events from the summer of 2013 to January 2015 were to change my way of thinking and believing entirely.

The burden of proof was now not something I could prove factually or in court.

Seeking proper context, I will begin at the beginning and go back in time more than 60 years to when I was still a small toddler, playing in my bedroom in our two storey family home near Hull, an industrial port in the East Riding of Yorkshire.

Our family home in Hull between 1957 and 1960

Now it is only looking back at that time, with adult hindsight, that one event which happened there takes on a new significance.

I guess I was only about two or three years old, but the memory has always remained fresh.

While playing on the floor in my back bedroom on a warm sunny day, I suddenly heard a strange noise outside. As any inquisitive child might do, and ignoring my mother's instructions to never lean out of an open window, I climbed onto the wooden chair in my room and peered outside. I looked down and saw nothing. Then I glanced to my right to see the unfamiliar hairy arms of someone emptying a large wooden pot of faeces out of a neighbouring window. The vision was truly scary. I yelped and jumped down from the chair onto the soft carpet of my bedroom.

The room from where I saw the pot being emptied was our bathroom. But there was only mum and I in the house, and mum was downstairs in the kitchen. My young brain screamed for an explanation.

I began to cry and called for my mother to tell her what I had seen. Within seconds I could hear her running upstairs and I still remember her chastising me for climbing on a chair to look out of my window and ordering me never to do it again as it was dangerous and I might fall.

"You were probably dreaming," she said, as she closed the window. But the worried and enquiring look on her face that afternoon stayed with me.

The second relevant experience happened about four years later. Following the birth of my sister Joanne in January 1959, my family moved to an old Victorian semi-detached house in Shoreham-by-Sea in Sussex, some 265 miles south of Hull.

Shoreham was a quiet backwater of a port town a few miles west of Brighton. It was also home to my maternal grandparents.

It was the spring of 1961, I was five years old and at home, off school, with a high fever and tonsillitis. I was sick and sweating, waiting for the doctor to arrive and mum had made me a bed in the front living room, so she could keep an eye on me.

As I waited I stared out of the ground floor sash window and gasped as I suddenly saw a man walking across the street wearing a strange long brown leather coat and dark Donald Duck type mask.

He was carrying a large bag and a long stick and was striding purposefully in the direction of our house.

The new family home in Gordon Road, Shoreham by Sea, Sussex

I quickly jumped under the sheets of my temporary bed and lay quietly. But nothing happened. So lying still I waited, and waited some more.

Then after about half an hour the doctor arrived... a bespectacled man in a tweed jacket, a white shirt and a tie. He took my temperature, listened to my chest and then gave my mother a prescription for antibiotics. He looked down at me and told me to rest and be a good boy.

I nodded my head and coughed.

Then in my young mind I puzzled: who had I seen in the street with the Donald Duck mask and long leather coat?

It was broad daylight and the vision was strange but real and it has stayed with me ever since.

Only when I went to high school some seven years later did a peculiar revelation hit me. During a history lesson I learned that before proper sanitation, between the 14th and 17th centuries, people would throw their waste excrement into the street, often from upstairs windows.

I also learned that physicians or 'quacks' wore long leather coats and duck-like masks during outbreaks of the Plague. The beak was filled with pot-pourri to cover the stench of the dying and the rotting dead. And they would also often carry a long stick with a globe of more pot-pourri hanging at the end.

On learning this I immediately recalled the visions of my very young years and since puzzled about them often as I grew older.

Now as I piece together this book, historical research casts some interesting light, which will become more relevant as you read further into this story.

A Plague or Quack doctor similar to my vision

During the second half of the 14th century (from the winter of 1348-49), up to half of the population of Britain were wiped out by the Black Death – a bubonic and pneumonic Plague initially spread by rats on trading ships from South Asia. Across Europe the Black Death accounted for more than 43 million deaths.

Port towns such as Shoreham suffered as badly - or worse - as any place in the rest of England.

Records show a settlement had existed at Shoreham as far back as Roman times, when the local River Adur flowed straight out to sea. Ships carrying soldiers fresh from the continent called at Portus Adurni on the river to pick up a pilot, before proceeding up river to the Roman village at Steyning – some six miles north - which had a road connection to London.

Shoreham harbour itself started to become important during the time of the Normans. For 300 years after the Norman Conquest of 1066 a great deal of trade between Shoreham and Normandy made the harbour the major route to and from the continent.

It also became a conduit for disease.

The town had gained a considerable reputation for ship building. In 1346, 26 boats were commissioned to be built at Shoreham for the blockade of Calais during the 100 Years War with France. The anchorage for these wooden ships was in the river just off the town quay.

It seems likely that one of the returning merchantmen came back to Shoreham carrying the Black Death in 1347-48, which then spread to wreak havoc on the whole country.

The main spread of the disease in England was from ports on the south coast such as Shoreham. The so-called *Cinque Ports* of Sandwich, Dover, Hythe, New Romney, Hastings, Winchelsea and Rye were other starting points, and the disease radiated out along the main trade routes to London and beyond.

I have not located any exact mortality records for Shoreham as formal parish records did not exist at this time, but it is certain that the town was hit hard and more than 60% of its population were lost to the Plague – Sussex as a whole endured a mortality of at least 50%.

Hull as an important northern port similarly suffered from the Black Death of 1348-49, which probably killed about half of its 6,500 population.

But as regards Hull, my toddler vision actually had little to do with the Black Death and much more to do with sanitation.

Historical records show that by the standards of medieval England, Hull was already a large and important commercial port and its streets were paved with stone. *"But without central sanitation and over-crowded living, they were no doubt very dirty, full of animal dung, human faeces and other refuse,"* reports British History Online (BHO).

Had my childhood visions been snapshots from a previous life? Or were they memories locked in inherited DNA from my ancestors? Or even trapped like video tape in the magnetic ferrous iron traces of the walls and masonry of the buildings where we lived, and then replayed like a hologram when triggered by negative emotions?

I do not know. But a series of unconnected events during 2013 and 2014 made me revisit these earlier memories with a completely new perspective.

Chapter Two
The Rose Garden

"The thing I find really scary about ghosts and demons is that you don't really know what they are or where they are. They're not very well understood. You don't know what they want from you. Anything that's unknown and mysterious is very scary."
Oren Peli

In 2012 my life was about to change in ways I could never have imagined.

After a lifetime as a successful journalist, and more recently, seven consecutive years as editor of a weekly county newspaper in North Wales, plus being a single father of a vibrant pre-teen boy, my life had become a routine of work, child care and domesticity.

Then with my 11-year-old son Nathan as best man, in February 2013 I married a lovely woman named Gill. We had bonded since first meeting the previous year and she made me feel more content at home and with my life in general than I had been for a very long while.

We began building our new family together and I marvelled as she became a natural and generous step-mother to my son as we developed a new and quite diverse routine to our lives.

At work, my job editing the local county newspaper was marking time as I edged into later middle age. At home weekends were full of adventure and as a family of three we began to plan the future and importantly Nathan's move up to high school the following autumn.

But as John Lennon once wrote: *"Life is what happens when you're busy making other plans"* and everything was about to change well beyond any plans we were making.

On the back of our marriage and a need to minimise the 65 miles between our two homes in Wales and Wolverhampton, we decided to relocate our home in time for Nathan's change of schools and to also ease commuting to and from work.

In May 2013 Gill and I signed to rent an old cottage in the sleepy Shropshire market town of Whitchurch. The cottage was just 40 miles from Gill's place of work at Wolverhampton University and 33 miles from my newspaper office in Mold.

By the beginning of June we had already visited the cottage twice over and really fallen in love with its quirky layout and unique character.

Our home at The Nurseries in the village of Cymau, North Wales

In the meantime, we stayed ensconced in my large detached house at The Nurseries (a cul-de-sac of 1990s built houses) in the tiny village of Cymau in the North Wales' hills, while making regular visits to Gill's Victorian semi in Wolverhampton. For weeks of that early summer we were perched like two flightless birds amid a host of packing cases and rolls of parcel tape and paper, while juggling the daily routines of work and school.

Then on the evening of Tuesday 4th June, with Nathan playing upstairs in his bedroom, Gill and I settled down to watch, for the very first time, the 2005 supernatural horror movie *The Exorcism of Emily Rose*. We had spontaneously bought the DVD the previous weekend while visiting Whitchurch.

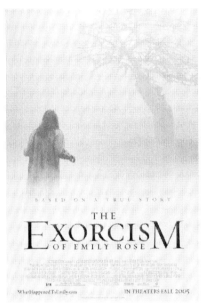

The Exorcism of Emily Rose

    The plot is detailed, but it is key to much of what happened next. In brief, this is the story of the movie:

    Emily Rose, a 19-year-old American teenager, played by Jennifer Carpenter (of Dexter fame), dies of self-inflicted wounds and malnutrition following an attempted Christian exorcism. Father Richard Moore, a Catholic diocesan priest, played by Tom Wilkinson, who attempted the exorcism, is arrested and sent to court.

    Erin Bruner, played by Laura Linney, an ambitious lawyer, takes on the case. Moore agrees to let her defend him if he can tell the truth behind Emily's story.

    During the trial, Emily's past is told through flashbacks and the evidence provided by witnesses, with Ethan Thomas, a practising Methodist, serving as prosecutor. He claims Emily suffered from epilepsy and psychosis to explain her behaviour. Emily received a scholarship to study for a bachelor's degree but displayed signs of demonic possession after she began attending classes, and experienced visions and physical contortions.

13

Diagnosed with epilepsy, Emily received anti-seizure medication but the treatment failed to cure her. Emily returns to her family home, where she continues displaying traits of possession until Moore was summoned to attempt an exorcism.

Meanwhile during the trial, Bruner begins experiencing supernatural phenomena at home, waking up at 3am to the smell of burning material. Moore warns her she may also be a target for the demons, revealing he too had experienced similar phenomena on the night he was preparing the exorcism.

With the prosecution building a strong case, Bruner summons Graham Cartwright, a medical doctor who attended the exorcism. He gives Bruner a cassette tape on which the exorcism is recorded.

Moore is called to the stand where he plays the tape. As seen in a flashback, Moore, Emily's father, a friend Jason, and Dr Cartwright participate in the exorcism while her mother and sisters pray in the living room.

At home in Cymau and relaxing on our sofa it was getting dark and both Gill and I were totally engrossed in the film.

On the TV screen the Rev Moore (Tom Wilkinson) begins reciting an exorcism in Latin as the characters try to lay to rest the demon inhabiting Emily Rose.

But then movie fantasy became a sudden reality… the DVD inside the player instantly froze for 10 seconds and spontaneously both Gill and I smelled the distinctive scent of fresh roses. There were no flowers in our house and neither of us were wearing perfume or after-shave.

It was bizarre.

We both stared at each other and noted the moment.

We continued watching the movie to its conclusion, but punctuated our viewing by a kind of *"what the hell was that?"* discussion which continued over a mug of cocoa in bed.

The following day, 'bizarre' became a bit frightening, when through an online investigation via Google searches we discovered the scent of roses often accompanies the passing of a spirit into the 'other world'.

We further discovered that the words recited in the movie were read verbatim by Tom Wilkinson from a true Latin script on Christian exorcism.

DE EXORCIZANDIS

OBSESSIS A DÆMONIO.

Sacerdos, sive quivis alius legitimus Ecclesia minister, vexatos à dæmone exorcizaturus, ea qua par est pietate, prudentia, ac vitæ integritate præditus esse debet, qui non sua, sed divina fretus virtute, ab omni rerum humanarum cupiditate alienus, tam pium opus ex charitate constanter et humiliter exequatur. Hunc præterea maturæ ætatis esse decet, et non solùm officio, sed etiam morum gravitate reverendum.

Ut igitur suo munere rectè fungatur, cùm alia multa sibi utilia documenta, quæ brevitatis gratiâ hoc loco prætermittuntur, ex probatis Authoribus, et ex usu noscere studeat, tum hæc pauca magis necessaria diligenter observabit.

In primis, ne facilè credat, aliquem à dæmonio obsessum esse; sed nota habeat ea signa, quibus obsessus dignoscitur ab iis, qui vel atra bile, vel morbo aliquo laborant. Signa autem obsidentis dæmonis sunt: Ignota lingua loqui pluribus verbis, vel loquentem intelligere; Distantia, et occulta patefacere; Vires supra ætatis, seu conditionis naturam ostendere; et id genus alia, quæ cùm plurima concurrunt, majora sunt indicia.

Hæc autem ut magis cognoscat, post unum, aut alterum exorcismum interroget obsessum ...

quid senserit in animo, vel in corpore, ut sciat etiam ad quænam verba magis diaboli conturbentur, ut ea deinceps magis inculcet ac repetat.

Advertat, quibus artibus ac deceptionibus utantur dæmones ad Exorcistam decipiendum: solent enim ut plurimùm fallaciter respondere, et difficilè se manifestare, ut Exorcista diu defatigatus desistat; aut infirmus videatur non esse à dæmonio vexatus.

Aliquando postquam sunt manifesti, abscondunt se, et relinquunt corpus quasi liberum ab omni molestia, ut infirmus putet se omninò esse liberatum; sed cessare non debet Exorcista, donec viderit signa liberationis.

Aliquando etiam dæmones ponunt quæcumque possunt impedimenta, ne infirmus se subjiciat exorcismis, vel conantur persuadere infirmitatem esse naturalem; interdum in medio exorcismi faciunt dormire infirmum, et ei visionem aliquam ostendunt, subtrahendo se, ut infirmus liberatus videatur.

Aliqui ostendunt factum maleficium, et à quibus sit factum, et modum ad illud dissipandum; sed caveat, ne ob hoc ad magos, vel ad sagas, vel ad alios; quàm ad Ecclesiæ ministros confugiat, aut ulla superstitione, aut alio modo illicito utatur.

Quandoque diabolus infirmum quiescere, et suscipere sanctissimam Eucharistiam permittit, ut discessisse videatur.

Denique innumerabiles sunt artes et fraudes diaboli ad decipiendum hominem, quibus ne fallatur, Exorcista cautus esse debet.

Quare memor Dominum nostrum dixisse, genus esse dæmoniorum, quod non ejicitur nisi per

The script of a genuine Latin Christian exorcism as used in the movie *The Exorcism of Emily Rose*

Genuinely shaken, we laughed it off as something weird and unexplained as we continued with our packing for our big house move.

But two days later the events of that Tuesday movie evening suddenly took on a new dimension. On Friday afternoon (7th June) while shopping in the local Asda supermarket, and by sheer chance, I bumped into Bryn, the father of Cameron, one of Nathan's friends from his weekly taekwondo sessions. We had not spoken for a few weeks and we stood in the CD and music aisle chatting about all kinds of things… cars, football, school and our respective boys' progress at taekwondo. I mentioned Gill and our pending house move and invited Bryn and his wife over for a farewell drink.

Suddenly he asked: *"Whereabouts in Cymau do you live?"*

I told him our address and Bryn's eyes widened.

"Ah that used to be a large rose nursery many years ago… which is probably why they named the road The Nurseries," he volunteered with a slight laugh.

"My grandfather worked there as a gardener and I used to love playing there when I was a kid," he continued.

"I remember there was a small orchard there and a few family graves way back in the 1980s," he added.

I can't recall my exact reply, but I do remember staring at his mouth moving while trying to understand what he had just told me. His words still remain lodged in my brain. And they bothered me as I drove home to relay the news to Gill, who was similarly surprised and slightly intrigued.

"It might explain things," she said, *"but quite what, is beyond me."*

I agreed and we both went to bed that night talking further about the Emily Rose movie and the events of the Tuesday evening.

But our spiritual intrigue and house move preparations were about to be side-swiped by something far more serious and totally unexpected.

Exactly eight days after watching **The Exorcism of Emily Rose**, life events took a whole new turn. That turn was to be truly life-changing.

Following a few months of quite stressful office politics at work, on the morning of Wednesday 12th June I walked into my newspaper office at 8am to find that one of the younger associate editors, some 15 years my junior, had dramatically changed the front page of my paper after I had gone to press and without the courtesy of a phone call or any reference back to me. As a hardened hack, I had never seen this happen during my whole career in the industry.

In a blur of fury and helplessness at that moment an elastic band inside me snapped. I flipped and began crying. I spontaneously left the office and drove the short distance home to the sanctuary of my family.

I was later told I had suffered a minor 'nervous breakdown' and it was probably caused by a series of life crises, the stress of work and our impending family relocation.

Within 24 hours, with our house move due in a fortnight, I was being treated by my GP for depression and anxiety, signed off work for at least two months and prescribed an antidepressant drug with the trade name Sertraline.

Meanwhile, we had no idea about what the next few months would bring us.

But now looking back with 20-20 hindsight everything that happened up to that point in time had a purpose and everything would eventually knit together in the narrative that follows.

In 2013 I felt I was touching the void. But six years later as I write this book, that void has filled up with discovery, not only about myself, but also about the world we live in.

Seemingly unconnected events are now connected.

Chapter Three
The Hole

"I have seen many storms in my life. Most storms have caught me by surprise, so I had to learn very quickly to look further and understand that I am not capable of controlling the weather, to exercise the art of patience and to respect the fury of nature."
Paulo Coelho

Plympton Cottage in Tarporley Road, Whitchurch

Two days after my breakdown, on Friday 14th June, with the steadying hand of Gill by my side, we drove to the estate agents office in Wrexham and collected the keys for our new home in Whitchurch.

The house removal was set for Friday 28th June and we only had last minute packing, cleaning and postal redirection notices to attend to.

Whitchurch is the northernmost market town in Shropshire, sitting on the borders of south Cheshire and Wales. With a population of just 9,700, it is comfortably self-sufficient for almost everything, with a raft of independent shops, friendly pubs and cafes, a cottage hospital, a high school and primary school, three annual town festivals and a thriving community. It is just two miles from the Welsh border, 20 miles from Shrewsbury and Chester and 18 miles from Wrexham.

It is probably a good idea to give a little historical background to this town which would become our home for the next 18 months...

Although there is no written history of early times, there is evidence from various discovered flint artefacts that people had lived here from about 3,000 BC.

Whitchurch lies on the A41/A49 Roman (Watling Street) Road and is the only town in Shropshire built on an original Roman site. A selection of Roman burial vases were excavated during refurbishments in the town's High Street in the early 1980s, leading experts to believe that this was a cemetery site below a fort at the top of the street.

Many more Roman artefacts have since been unearthed in the aptly named Roman Way, beyond the top of High Street and adjacent to Bargates, where our new home Plympton Cottage has stood for over 170 years.

After the Norman Conquest in 1066, Whitchurch's location on the Welsh marches would require the Lords of Westune (the Saxon name for Whitchurch) to engage in constant military activity against attacks from the Welsh. A motte and bailey castle and a new white Grinshill stone church were both built at the crest of what is now known as Bargates, and Westune soon became known as Album Monasterium (White Church).

The town was granted market status in the 14th Century. A replacement third church collapsed in July 1711 and the present Queen Anne parish church of St Alkmund was constructed to take its place.

In the 18th Century, many of the earlier timber-framed buildings were refaced in more fashionable brick. New elegant Georgian houses were also built at the southern end of the High Street.

The oldest building in Whitchurch is the *Old Eagles* pub in Watergate Street. It was probably built during the 14th century but only became a pub in 1868. There are other half-timbered buildings alongside and further up the street.

The High Street has many old buildings many of which are older than their replacement Georgian frontages would suggest.

In short, Whitchurch reeks history at every turn, and that history would come to haunt us again and again.

The location of Plympton Cottage alongside neighbouring properties

Our new home was originally called Cottage Number 1, before being aptly renamed Plympton Cottage by one of its owners after he was demobbed from the First World War trenches to a hospital at Plympton near Plymouth in Devon.

This small cottage attached via a stone alley to a much larger 18th century building named Bargates House to its right, while next door to the left is an even larger and more modern detached house named The Gables. Our cottage had obviously been built and extended in at least three tranches - from an original 18th century structure - separated by many years between each.

It provided us with a deceptive and well-proportioned period property, with two reception rooms, a conservatory, kitchen, bathroom and three bedrooms with a long narrow garden to the rear.

The cottage is situated adjacent to a roundabout at the intersection of Bargates (the continuation of the town's High Street) and the main north-leading Tarporley Road.

The immediate area around us had been the site of a number of archaeological excavations. Two seasons of excavation were carried out by Barri Jones of Manchester University in August 1965 and April 1966. The work was prompted by a re-development scheme affecting the area forming the western edge of the town

An archaeological report of the works includes specialist reports on pottery, coins, metalwork and animal bones from the site, and a report on a 'trepanned skeleton' discovered beneath the floor level of one building.

But more about this later…

Meanwhile, in June 2013, despite continuing worries about my fragile mental health, Gill and I were excited and began moving bits and pieces from Cymau to the cottage and undertaking some cleaning in preparation for the big move.

On Tuesday 18th June, I bought a set of gorgeous old pitch pine shelves for our kitchen. They were perfect for displaying my wife's collection of old blue and white TG Green Cornishware pottery.

That afternoon, using my electric drill and four 3½ inch screws, I attached the shelves to the end wall in our new kitchen. Once in place the shelves looked perfect, so I began packing away my tools and cleaning up the dust from the drill holes.

Then, without any warning, a large jar of screws – which I had kept for over 30 years – suddenly slipped through my hands and smashed all over the quarry-tiled kitchen floor, scattering screws and broken glass almost everywhere.

I cursed as I cleaned up the mess, trying not to cut my hands on the broken glass. But I thought nothing more of it other than it was just a simple accident.

"Must be the Sertraline, making me clumsy," I said quietly to myself. Although I couldn't be sure.

But this was just the beginning.

On Friday 28th June, we finally moved house… and events took yet another serious and totally unexpected turn. It was as if

21

someone, or something, else was conducting both our lives in succession.

After watching the removal team spend a couple of hours packing their truck with all our furniture and possessions at my old house in Cymau, we set off in our respective cars to make the 25 mile journey to Whitchurch.

At about 2pm, on an overcast summer's afternoon, the removal lorry arrived outside our new cottage and with the threat of rain, Gill and I made ourselves busy by carrying a few boxes through the body of the cottage to the conservatory and shed at the back. We left the removal professionals to carry all the furniture and heavy boxes.

About 20 minutes into our work and with a spitting of light summer rain, it suddenly happened… a few feet behind me, Gill screamed in agony as she fell into a small but hidden hole in our back lawn. We had visited the cottage at least half a dozen times, but neither of us had ever seen this hole before.

Gill's left knee had twisted backwards and she was unable to move and lay there on the damp grass crying in pain.

Panic ensued. I immediately telephoned for an ambulance. Gill was clearly in agony and as the rain fell harder I tried to keep her warm and dry.

Luckily a paramedic in a hatchback ambulance car arrived within 10 minutes and he quickly ascertained that Gill had probably broken her left leg.

A further 20 minutes passed before an ambulance arrived on the scene, and after some problems carrying her on a stretcher through the twisty and stepped cottage, the ambulance crew rushed Gill to our nearest major hospital some 18 miles away in Shrewsbury.

I tossed the house keys to the removal team and followed the ambulance in my car.

A few hours after arrival at the A&E department at the Royal Shrewsbury Hospital, the doctors diagnosed that Gill had ruptured the tendons around her left knee and broken the knee cap in the freak accident.

This major injury was all due to her falling into a small but previously unseen hole in the garden, in the middle of the lawn!

The hole where Gill broke her leg, before being filled in with earth

Gill's leg was set in plaster and she was prescribed six weeks of non-ambulant care at home while the complicated fracture mended itself.

After a few weeks the plaster was replaced by a lighter support contraption called a Genurange brace, which gave Gill some flexibility to at least get from the bed to the bathroom and back. But constant bed rest in the back bedroom of our new cottage followed for my poor wife during our hottest summer in 35 years.

Meanwhile, I gradually unpacked our belongings, filled drawers, cooked meals, put up pictures and curtains, did all the usual household chores and washed and bathed my immobile convalescent wife.

I also filled the hole in the lawn with stones and earth and searched the garden for anymore as yet undiscovered holes or booby traps. There were none.

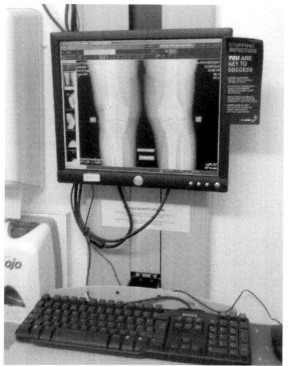

A hospital X Ray reveals Gill's broken left knee

Slowly during July and August life began piecing itself together.

But it was during this time I started to experience something very strange, which got stranger as the steaming hot summer weeks passed.

Plympton Cottage was cosy and above all full of character and charm, although parts of the centre of the building always felt a bit chilly… even in mid-summer.

Over the years, the cottage had been extended and undergone several alterations, including the transformation of a side passage, left of the front door, into the main body of the house, which in turn had allowed previous owners to enlarge the kitchen. Simple observations showed that the kitchen and adjoining living room were built at least two feet lower than the back garden and conservatory.

And it is in this extended area at the back of the kitchen where the unexplained started to occur.

It was the same area of the kitchen where I had dropped the jar of screws before the removal; I also dropped a plate full of food, a can of baked beans and numerous smaller items such as teaspoons and forks.

Before any reader suggests that my clumsiness might have been due to the doses of Sertraline I was taking, I soon discovered that this is not a recognised side-effect of the drug and certainly isn't the type of medication to prevent me driving or operating heavy machinery.

And it wasn't just me who was dropping things in this same small area of the house!

Chapter Four
The Drop Spirit Zone

"I believe that life is chaotic, a jumble of accidents, ambitions, misconceptions, bold intentions, lazy happenstances, and unintended consequences, yet I also believe that there are connections that illuminate our world, revealing its endless mystery and wonder."
David Maraniss

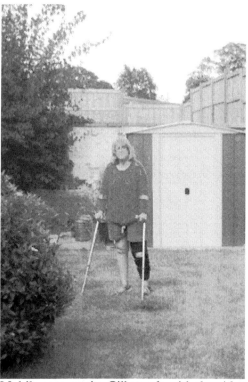

Mobile once again, Gill stands with the aid
of crutches by the hole where she broke her leg

By the beginning of September, with Nathan starting at the town's high school, Gill was gradually becoming mobile again, and with the help of a pair of crutches we managed to get out into town for a coffee and pizza.

26

And then twice a week, I drove her to the local cottage hospital for sessions of physiotherapy.

Two weeks into the month, we decided we were both strong enough to accept guests and invited my elderly mother to stay for a few days. She loved the cottage and immediately began helping with some light gardening and a few household chores.

Then after a few days, on one sunny autumn afternoon, while she was sitting at the kitchen table, I offered to show my mum Gill's prize piece of Cornishware pottery from the display shelves I had erected back in June.

The old pine display shelves with Gill's Cornishware pottery set inside the *Drop Spirit Zone*

It was a small blue and white striped Stilton cheese pot and was a piece of pottery we had recently acquired from an auction. I had handled the pot a few times, but on this occasion, as I was about to

27

hand it to my mother for closer inspection, its lid suddenly flew off and smashed on the kitchen floor.

It was another *'what happened there?'* moment.

My mother gasped.

"Is this where other things are breaking?" she asked in a puzzled and slightly nervous voice.

I bent down and picked up the pieces of smashed china and muttered *"Bloody hell, not again."*

It was after this event that we (Gill, Nathan, my mother, various visitors and I) began to note the regular array of accidents in this corner of the kitchen.

It was so strange that I started to diary each single event. The diary was partly to keep a practical log, but also to see if I could find any pattern to the time or place where each drop occurred.

Over the next 12 months, we individually and collectively dropped over 70 different items in this small area of the kitchen, including a glass of wine, a stack of baking tins, two soup bowls, an electric drill, a bag of frozen peas, a tray of cakes and a tub of spray cooking oil.

I also dropped and broke a mug, the lid from a valued china ginger jar, a sharp knife and a wooden box full of incense sticks in the zone... then without any warning our ironing board fell on my wife's head in the same area.

We nervously christened this part of the kitchen our *Drop Spirit Zone.*

We were genuinely intrigued, and at times a little frightened, by the spontaneous nature of the accidents, which always occurred in the same three metre square area at the back of the quarry tile floored kitchen, between the pantry door, the old pine table and the living room door.

What the hell was going on? We asked ourselves this almost every day.

In November 2013, I began some practical investigations into these unexplained occurrences... to be frank, we had no idea what we might discover.

One early winter evening, and with the lights turned off, I walked slowly into the darkened kitchen and as I passed the threshold from the adjoining living room I felt a vibration pass across my shoulders. I can only described the feeling as being like a jolt of electricity lasting no more than one second.

Looking from the Drop Spirit Zone to the doorway into the living room – notice the fridge/freezer to the left

I stood still. Suddenly a plastic pot of vitamin pills fell from the top of the adjacent fridge/freezer onto the floor behind me.

I jumped like a scared child.

Then events took another more sinister twist.

I took my expensive digital SLR camera to photograph the *Drop Spirit Zone* of the kitchen, hoping to catch something. As I held the camera ready to shoot, it fell, or rather leapt, from my grasp onto the floor.

I screamed in shock and looked round to see Gill watching me from the living room door.

Thankfully the phone was in a padded case and did not break.

But it didn't end there... on the morning of 19th November, Gill and I were drinking mugs of coffee while finishing our breakfast in the kitchen. I was sitting on one side of our old pine table with my back to the cooker and Gill was sitting at right angles three feet to the left of me.

We were talking blandly about the day ahead.

Suddenly, and without any warning, Gill's almost full mug of hot coffee leapt upwards in her hand and spilled down her clothes, scalding her lap. I looked at her amazed and gasped loudly. She returned the look with an added look of fear in her eyes.

Together, we mopped up the spilt coffee and checked she was not badly scalded.

I commented: *"Do you realise you are sitting in the Drop Spirit Zone?"*

"Yes," she replied. *"It was like some small hand suddenly pushed my mug upwards."*

A few seconds before the incident, Gill had just finished eating the last piece of bread on the table. As time passed, and in hindsight, it seemed the bread might be a key to the unexplained event.

Five weeks after the coffee mug incident, we were again eating breakfast at our kitchen table. Gill was sitting to my left – inside the *Drop Spirit Zone* – and I was sitting slightly outside it. Our old cat Frankie was sat on the quarry-tiled floor next to my wife.

Abruptly our normally docile and rather old Persian cat leapt into the air, meowed loudly and darted into the living room, where he hid under the coffee table. Gill and I stared at each other in amazement until we both uttered almost simultaneously: *"The Drop Spirit Zone!"*

From that moment Frankie stopped sitting on the floor in the kitchen, preferring to perch on our old pine settle to watch us eat breakfast or while away his morning.

Living and experiencing these unexpected events in our old cottage was by now becoming part of our daily lives.

But something else started to rattle our sense of the explained.

In early December 2013, after retiring upstairs to bed, we both began hearing strange sounds emanating from our kitchen.

Sitting bolt upright in bed, we would listen keenly. I often ventured downstairs in the small hours to check, but only ever found our cat asleep and nothing else that could be regarded as strange.

But from upstairs in our bedroom – immediately above the living room - it sounded as if our wooden kitchen chairs were being dragged across the quarry-tiled floor.

Once again: what the hell was going on?

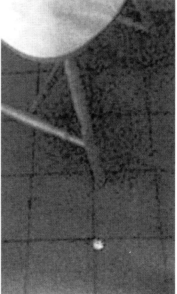

Our kitchen chair and marker experiment – notice the dramatic movement of both items overnight

This had gone beyond dropping objects and was becoming spooky and a little frightening.

Was the cottage haunted?

So we set up our own small experiment to try and clarify whether this was the case or whether it was all in our collective imagination.

Late one evening, Gill placed a small marker on the kitchen floor, next to a wooden chair which sat inside the Drop Spirit Zone. We also closed the living room door to ensure that our cat couldn't get into the kitchen.

We both retired to bed and waited.

That night, around 2am we heard the usual scraping sounds.

The next morning, to our amazement, we discovered the marker had moved about two inches from its spot... and the chair had moved over seven inches in a different direction!

Before and after photographs revealed the true extent of the movements.

Was our cottage haunted? Or was there some kind of supernatural possession which had followed us after the exorcism movie evening in my house in Cymau six months earlier?

Our own – and by the word 'our' I mean myself, my wife, my son and my mother – naturally sceptical natures were now being seriously challenged.

While we did not feel threatened by these unexplained events, we were deeply curious and determined to get to the bottom of it. Were there really ghosts or spirits at work here?

Our investigations began.

Chapter Five
Things that go Bump

"Our feet are planted in the real world, but we dance with angels and ghosts."
John Cameron Mitchell

A full week of online and local library research took us a little way forward in trying to understand what was happening.

According to widely acknowledged paranormal experts the most common of all ghosts spotted is usually of a deceased person, someone you might know, a family member or perhaps even a historical figure.

These ghosts often show themselves to others in a variety of different ways. They can become visible; they can speak or make noises, touch you or even emit an odour such as perfume, flowers or cigar smoke to let you know they are there.

Experts say that this type of ghost retains its former personality of when they were alive and can feel emotions. Often, they are visiting you to comfort you or let you know something important, claim these experts.

Quite different to a ghost, a poltergeist is said to have the ability to move or knock things over, make noises and manipulate the physical environment. But a poltergeist is actually one of the rarest forms of hauntings. Loud knocking sounds, lights turning on and off, doors slamming, even fires breaking out mysteriously have all been attributed to this type of spiritual disturbance. A frightening aspect of the poltergeist is that the events usually start out slowly and mildly, then begin to intensify.

Another supernatural phenomenon are known as orbs. Orbs are probably the most photographed type of spiritual anomaly. They appear as transparent or translucent balls of light hovering over the ground. They often make themselves known only after photographs have been developed or processed.

Some paranormal experts believe that orbs are the souls of a human, or even an animal, that has died and is traveling around from one place to another. The circular shape they take on makes it easier for them to move around and is often the first state they appear in before they become a full-bodied apparition. In photographs they are usually white but can be blue as well.

So were we haunted?

The scent of ghosts or spirits certainly had some resonance with our initial experience in Cymau some six months earlier, but the events in Plympton Cottage had all the different hallmarks of possible poltergeist activity.

Our investigations progressed as we started to enquire locally about any other recorded paranormal or unexplained happenings in our small market town.

Whitchurch Civic Centre – before its modernisation and new facade

A few years earlier the local newspaper reported that the phantom notes of a piano had been heard for several nights by a number of local people drifting from the unmanned *Whitchurch Civic Centre* in the high street, about 800 yards south of our cottage. An investigation at the time failed to find the source of the noise.

The town's oldest building: the Old Eagles pub in Watergate

Eight years earlier on 17th July 2005, at the *Old Eagles* pub in Watergate, on the other side of town, while the building was being investigated by a paranormal group, the voice of a young girl was recorded on video in the main cellar.

And *The Star Hotel* (now called *Percy's Bar*), in the town's Bull Ring is steeped in history. It was built around 1760 on the original sandstone walls of the medieval Watergate.

It was an old coaching inn and is widely claimed to be haunted by two men named William and Edward who show their displeasure when loud music is played and also when women dress inappropriately inside the Inn.

The Star Hotel (now known as Percy's Bar) in the town's Bull Ring

The Old Town Vaults in St Mary's Street

The *Whitchurch Paranormal Society* visited the venue, held a night time vigil and conducted an Ouija Board session. The Inn was described as *"very paranormally active"* by the ghost hunters.

The *Old Town Vaults* in St Mary's Street near the centre of town was first listed as an alehouse in 1823 and is also allegedly haunted by poltergeist activity and a phantom. At one time, there was an abattoir sited behind the pub, and ghost hunters believe this might have been the source of the *Old Town Vaults'* so-called phantom. One landlady saw a strange bearded figure in a leather apron, holding a large knife and dragging a bag, as she looked on through a bar window. She watched it for several seconds before it dissolved.

The Black Bear with St Alkmund's Church to the rear

Among the paranormal activities recorded are strong odours of perfume and tobacco. Lights have turned on and off, and employees having the strange feeling of being pushed as coincidentally they see a dark figure standing behind the bar.

Closer to home, the timber framed *Black Bear*, which lies at the top of Bargates, directly opposite St Alkmund's Church, dates back to 1662 and has been licensed since 1667. Two ghosts are reported to have taken up residence here, and both are frequently seen by staff and customers. One is an elderly man in a flat cap, sitting at a table in the bar. The other is a woman wearing a long dress, who walks through the bar at a rapid pace.

There have also been alleged paranormal activity and ghostly sightings at both the *White Bear* in the High Street and the *Cock and Greyhound* at the top of Bargates.

All truly fascinating!

But none of these places or events – with the exception of the *Old Town Vaults* - bore any resemblance or proximity to what we were experiencing inside Plympton Cottage, and all the so-called haunted buildings were also too far away geographically to seemingly have much relevance.

Our need to find out what was happening in our home was taking on a new urgency, and a poltergeist certainly seemed to be the most obvious answer to our paranormal experiences.

Some parapsychologists view poltergeists as a type of ghost or supernatural entity which is responsible for psychological and physical disturbances. Others believe that such activity originates from *'unknown energy'* associated with a living person or a location.

Poltergeist activity typically starts with minor isolated incidents. This could include unexplained sounds or familiar objects such as your keys or your phone moving from their usual place.

Some ghost hunters propose that poltergeists are actually the emotions of troubled individuals – built up during times of stress.

This theory, known as *Spontaneous Recurring Psychokinesis* suggests that this built-up stress then unconsciously projects outwards in the form of mental energy, which effects the physical environment and produces the phenomena attributed to poltergeists. But there is little evidence to support this notion.

Other people also believe that spirits of the dead are responsible for poltergeist activity. This is said to be because people who experience them perceive an underlying intelligence and meaningful communication with an otherworldly being.

So what was happening to us in our cottage?

Our initial investigations gave us a few ideas, but they were just hypotheses and nothing was yet certain.

We knew we had to dig deeper.

Chapter Six
A Series of Dreams

"Everything stays down where it's wounded
And comes to a permanent stop
Wasn't thinking of anything specific
Like in a dream, when someone wakes up and screams
Nothing too very scientific
Just thinking of a series of dreams"
Bob Dylan

Since we moved into Plympton Cottage the previous June my usual nightly sleep pattern had started to alter.

I had always been able to get off to sleep quickly and usually sleep quite soundly until about 6am. And if I ever had any dreams I only had vague flashes of them in my memory the next morning.

My first recurring dream:
Janet Brown (left) pictured circa
1962 with her friend Helen Swyer,
shortly before Janet's tragic death

But during the autumn/winter of 2013 I began to experience a vivid and recurring dream. It the first such dream I have had since I was a very small child when I was deeply traumatised after a girl named Janet Brown in my infant class in Shoreham was killed while crossing the main Old Shoreham road.

Janet was only six years old when she died, and the dreamscape images of meeting her at a white wicket gate with her green eyes and freckled face smiling at me as I bend down to pick up a half crown piece from the pavement and then fall headfirst into a dark tunnel became as clear as day. In my imagination, that image stayed with me forever. The dreams went on repeating themselves for many months and only stopped when our family moved house and I was transferred to a different primary school.

So to suddenly start experiencing another and different recurring dream at the age of 57 was, to be frank, quite shocking.

The new dream is plain in its simplicity and remained crystal clear, and just like the Janet dream years earlier, it played itself over again and again…

My second recurring dream: This photo is of a Victorian girl (she is actually a distant ancestor) similar in appearance to Edith.

I walk into our cottage kitchen alone at night and sit at the breakfast table. I look down at our cat in his basket which is placed close to the *Drop Spirit Zone*. Kneeling down alongside the cat is a

41

young girl, aged about seven years old. She is gently stroking our grey haired moggie.

The girl has unkempt brown hair with a cropped fringe, a freckled face and sad blue eyes. She is wearing a beige coloured straight Victorian style dress with a white ruff and a tie band around her waist. She looks up at me and says: *"I like cats."*

She tells me her name is Edith.

Then she asks me: *"Do you have any bread, Sir?"*

I stand up and walk to our bread crock on the worktop on the other side on the kitchen and retrieve a crust of thick-sliced white bread for her. When I return, the girl is running with her back to me into our pantry and down a steep staircase out of sight. It is at this point I awake, shaking with the images frozen in my mind.

The pantry door – Edith's dreamscape escape

42

I had this dream at least a dozen times over a period of three months. And questions over the significance of the dream from when Gill scalded herself with hot coffee after she had eaten the last piece of bread all those weeks earlier, began to run round my thoughts.

Then I started to also question what may have once existed beyond our pantry door, before the many conversions and extensions to the cottage had taken place. By looking at the array of different roof lines, the building had been altered and extended extensively during the previous 170 years to include the flat roofed kitchen, the side passageway, a modern conservatory and a division between the front and back of the cottage. And from recent information we also know that the blocking of the side passageway to the kitchen and the creation of the pantry (inside the *Drop Spirit Zone*), plus the creation of an open plan living and dining room, occurred more recently during extensive modernisation works to the cottage between 2002 and 2006.

So what once may have been a two roomed labourer's hovel had become over 150 years a cosy and spacious dwelling.

But the dream about Edith was just the beginning of what was to come.

It was early in the New Year when my dreamscape developed in the most bizarre way imaginable.

On the night of Sunday 12th January 2014, I experienced a different vivid dream in which I was helping four older men bury dead bodies in a huge ditch. My job in the dream was to shovel white powder over the bodies as they were thrown into a common grave. When I woke I recalled every part of the dream in detail and shared it with Gill.

The mens' names as they introduced themselves to me were Parcel, Barrow, Coppice and Venables. They appeared to have a foreman who they referred to as Mr Huddlestone.

The detail in the dream was precise and was like a movie playing itself out in real time in my sleeping subconscious.

Nina Kahn, author of *What Do Dreams About Ghosts Mean?* says: *"Dreams that involve contact with a ghost or spirit are also known as visitation dreams, and they're actually quite common. They can be striking emotionally intense dreams in which a recently deceased loved one returns to provide guidance, reassurance, and/or warning.*

"So if an apparition is actually contacting you in your sleep, you'll know, as it'll feel distinctly different than your average dream.

"And according to many psychics and paranormal experts, when it comes to visitation dreams, we shouldn't expect science to explain it away, as dreams are considered one of the most effective ways for the spirit realm to connect to the living.

"While sleeping, your conscious mind has quietened and you have less resistance through your own thoughts, blockages and beliefs — you're relaxed and open.

"This makes sense, if you think about it. During a dream state, we've left our conscious, rational mind behind and are more open to symbolism or fantastical events — and possibly more open to the spiritual, too," she adds.

"It is actually easier for spiritual entities of all kinds to communicate with us while we are sleeping," explains Dr Anne Reith, founder of **The Institute for Mediumship, Psychic, Astrological, and Reiki Training**. *"So if a spirit has a message for you, maybe it's aware that you're more likely to be receptive to it in a dream than you would be in a waking state."*

Apparently, though, it isn't just loved ones who can visit you during a dream state.

"Any spirit can get in touch with you while you sleep," explains psychic medium Amanda Linette Meder, in her **Spiritual Living** blog.

"This includes people that you know who have crossed over, other deceased people that you have yet to meet but want to get your attention."

And while many reports of visitation dreams are overwhelmingly positive, there are certainly times when they could be more sinister. So-called 'earthbound spirits' are allegedly ghosts who have remained behind due to an attachment or fear of passing on. These are typically the ghosts that are attributed to hauntings — and they can sometimes make their way into people's dreams.

But exactly what was triggering my dreams about people I didn't know and who seemingly didn't exist?

Were my dreams drug-induced by the daily doses of the antidepressant Sertraline?

Certainly, according to the leaflet which came with the medication, some of the recognised side-effects from taking 100 mg of Sertraline a day may include: a change in sleep habits, increased sleepiness and insomnia plus hallucinations or vivid dreams.

So was all this just imagination and were my dreams in any way linked to the unexplained occurrences within our cottage – witnessed by other people?

I needed to do a bit more digging.

I had once been a psychiatric nurse when I was much younger, so finding information and resources online was quite straightforward.

Sertraline has a molecular formula of $C_{17}H_{17}Cl_2N$ and is a type of antidepressant known as a selective serotonin reuptake inhibitor (SSRI) which interrupts synapses in the brain. The drug is commonly prescribed to treat depression, and sometimes panic attacks, obsessive compulsive disorder (OCD) and post-traumatic stress disorder (PTSD).

It has many properties and side-effects linked in parallel to the illegal hallucinogenic Ayahuasca.

And this is where my investigations became quite fascinating.

Ayahuasca is a herbal drink made from plants that grow in the Amazon jungle. For centuries, this tea has been used in healing ceremonies. The drink causes hallucinations and is said to have spiritual and therapeutic benefits. In recent years, it has attracted the attention of Western medicine as a possible treatment for depression. The drug has also become popular with people seeking a *'Shaman experience'* and many Amazonian tribes use it in rituals to talk to their dead ancestors.

According to the journal **Nature**, a booming industry has developed in South America, as thousands of people pay big money to attend retreats so they can sample Ayahuasca's *'intense psychedelic insights.'*

The recipe for Ayahuasca — also spelled iowaska or hoasca, and also called daime, yajé, yagé, natema and vegetal — differs by region, according to the **Journal of Pharmacology**. In Brazil, Peru and Ecuador, pounded stems of a flowering vine (Banisteriopsis caapi) are used to make the teas, either alone or combined with the leaves of a shrub (Psychotria viridis). In Ecuador and Colombia, the stems of B. caapi are combined with a different shrub (Diplopterys cabrerana).

The tea is prepared by an *Ayahuasquero*, who serves the drink during a ceremony that usually takes place in a Shaman's hut.

Those partaking in the tea lie on grass mats or mattresses while riding out the high, which can last for hours. The Ayahuasca tea is used to bring on a "mental awakening" and a psychic connection to the living and the dead.

In a 2014 article for ***Live Science***, contributor Benjamin Radford cited a passage from the book ***Magic and Witchcraft: From Shamanism to the Technopagans***: *"Taking this sacrament allows the shaman to enter the supernatural realm, to have initiatory visions, and to make contact with ancestors and helper-spirits."*

While Western medicine has known about Ayahuasca for around 100 years, little is known about how it works. Ayahuasca contains Dimethyltryptamine (DMT or N, N-DMT), which is a psychedelic compound that causes intense hallucinations. It is found in many plants, and it is also the only psychedelic known to occur naturally in the human body, according to a ***Scientific American*** article.

So had the Sertraline I was taking opened up synapses in my semi-conscious brain while sleeping and made invisible connections to the past or even to spirits inhabiting our home – in much the same way that Ayahuasca is claimed to do?

Or did my own Near Death Experience (NDE) some 25 years earlier, when I medically died for 10 minutes on a hospital operating table while undergoing surgery for lung cancer, trigger an open synapse response to the spirits?

I am unsure and the questions and hypotheses still remain unanswered.

But while pondering the cause of my dreams with Gill and close friends, events took yet another turn which gave a brave new world insight into everything that had happened over the previous six months.

Chapter Seven
Skeleton Keys

"The past is dead and buried. But I know now that buried things have a way of rising to the surface when one least expects them to."
Dan Simmons

The back of Plympton Cottage, showing the raised garden and patio and the modern conservatory well above the level of the kitchen

Everything about our time in Plympton Cottage was becoming a never-ending rollercoaster of unexplained events and discoveries.

But nothing came close to what happened on Monday 13th January 2014.

What occurred that day became a true *"Oh My God"* pivotal moment that will stay with me until the day I die.

While sitting in my small front office on the first floor of our cottage I was sipping coffee and making a few random internet fishing exercises on the history of Whitchurch and more specifically the area where our cottage was built.

Suddenly, I discovered through Shropshire County Council's online archives that our house and garden lie on a 'cemetery of unknown origin'. The archive states that there had been an archaeological excavation sometime during the previous 70 years and seven extended skeletons were discovered in the grounds of our house!

The document that was to shake us to our bones

The document *(HER Number (PRN): 00914)* states:
Inhumations In Grounds Of The Gables and Plympton, Whitchurch: probable Inhumation Cemetery (Roman) at Grid Reference: SJ 5397 4193, Brief

Description: Seven extended skeletons are reported to have been found here sometime before 1950, yet the inhumation revealed no archaeological deposits.

It further notes that a 1976 review of the findings in the immediate rear garden of Plympton Cottage, added the fact that the owner of the cottage, *"who had lived there for 35 years"* had never heard of the burials.

Yet the recognised enclosed Roman cemetery is about 600 yards south of the cottage near the Roman wall at the top of Bargates towards the town centre.

I think I screamed something like *"What the hell is this?"* quite loudly as I sat in my office while reading and re-reading this document. Then I printed out three A4 copies to prove I wasn't hallucinating!

I was shaking and absorbed in a sense of total incredulity that this was real.

Over the next half an hour I telephoned Gill at work at Wolverhampton University to tell her of my finding and could hear her gasp of *"You must be joking!"* before I emailed her the evidence.

I then rang my mum at her home in North Wales. She was similarly shocked and disbelieving.

After another strong coffee, my next port of call was to telephone the Shropshire County archives in Shrewsbury. I was transferred between one department and another before I eventually spoke with an expert at Shropshire Council Environment History Team.

Following a brief conversation and explaining that I actually lived at Plympton Cottage, the young sounding guy kindly promised to do some research on the document's findings and ring me back. He warned that it would probably take at least 24 hours.

So I waited.

And sure enough, at about 11am the next morning (Tuesday 14th January) the man telephoned me to say he had looked at the files surrounding various excavation work at our address.

From simple deductions around the time frames of various reports, it appears that the seven skeletons were unearthed sometime before 1950, possibly while the foundations were being dug for the kitchen extension at our cottage… the same quarry tiled kitchen where all our unexplained occurrences had been taking place!

At the time of the excavations, the skeletons were thought to be Roman remains as that seemed most logical, given the Roman history of the town. But that was just a best guess or assumption by the archaeologists. As there was no Carbon 14 dating techniques before 1950, there was no way to precisely date how old the skeletons were.

One shared hypothesis between us was that it may have been a Plague related burial, possibly dating from a huge outbreak of bubonic Plague in the town in 1650 or an even earlier burial ground from when the Black Death visited the town in the 14th century.

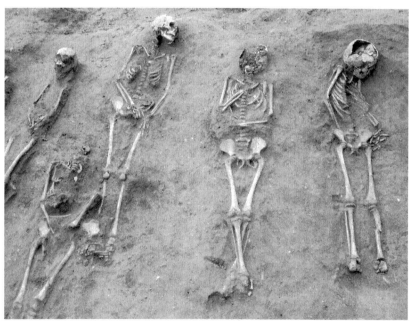

Extended skeletons as recovered from a 14th century Plague (Black Death) burial in Lincolnshire

But what was the real origin of these skeletons and where were they now?

Clearly puzzled, the council archivist said there was no way of knowing what had happened to the skeletons when they were unearthed. He thought they might have been given a Christian burial in the local churchyard OR left in place. The council's Environment History Team had no record about what became of them.

As the discovery was made either during or just after World War II, it is likely that local authority resources were stretched to the limit and little attention would have been given to seven historical skeletons at a time when burial space for thousands of recently deceased people was at a premium.

And without further excavation work there was no way of knowing how many more there were – or are - still buried.

The origin of the skeletons and their final resting place was now the great unknown.

With heart-stopping interest as an investigative journalist and a historian, I undertook further internet searches.

I discovered that during the English Civil War, Cromwell's Parliamentary forces of 800 men under the command of Sir William Brereton took Whitchurch on 30th May 1643. A bloody skirmish took place about 500 yards east of our cottage adjacent to what is now Claypit Street. Some 28 soldiers and three prisoners were killed.

The mass of graves at Whitchurch Cemetery

The Parish Register records the burial of the soldiers and prisoners on that date, although the records do not say where any of them were actually buried.

One would assume that as serving soldiers they would have been afforded a Christian burial on consecrated ground. So it was highly unlikely they would be interred in the ground of our cottage.

Then, with Gill's help, I began to scour the 3,400 graves a mile away at Whitchurch Cemetery in Mile Bank Road, which was opened in 1885, and the expansive older graveyard at the nearby St Alkmund's Church.

St Alkmund's Church at the top of Bargates

I even telephoned Rev Canon Judy Hunt, the rector of the church. She had no knowledge of the skeleton finds, but confirmed they were not, to the best of her knowledge, buried in her churchyard.

These searches among the town's graves led to the next heart-stopping discovery... Purcell, Barrow, Coppage, Venables and Huddlestone are/were all common surnames in the town.

We also found the grave of an eight-year-old girl called Edith!

It was yet another *"What the hell is going on?"* moment. How come those names and the burials occurred in my dreams before I had any knowledge of any of them?

The unexplained had become unexplainable.

Were spirits really invading my sleeping senses?

On Wednesday 15th January 2014 another huge surprise was awaiting me.

I walked into town and decided to make some enquiries at the local Heritage Centre – run by volunteers and amateur historians. I quietly enquired at the reception desk about whether they had any documentary evidence about the discovery of skeletons at Plympton Cottage or The Gables.

Whitchurch Heritage Centre

With a shrug of her shoulders the receptionist said it was the first she had heard of it and suggested I telephone the county archives in Shrewsbury – which of course I had already done! An older member of staff confirmed that this was the first time she had ever heard of this claim of burials at the foot of Tarporley Road.

Then something amazing happened.

I was suddenly and quietly ushered away to a corner of the centre by another female member of the Heritage Centre staff. The lady seemed both excited and interested.

"Did you say Plympton Cottage?" she asked.

I confirmed my address and she appeared almost dumbstruck as her eyes widened and wanted to know more about the skeletons. So I told her all I knew from the archive documents I had first seen 48 hours earlier.

The spectacled lady stuttered slightly as she told me she used to live in the same cottage. She turned to ensure no-one overheard us before quietly saying that she loved the cottage, but the reason she moved out was she believed it was haunted. She spoke at length about objects dropping to the floor, mirrors and pictures falling from the wall, objects disappearing and the sound of footsteps on the landing when no one else was in the house. *"My son said he kept seeing a man standing in his bedroom,"* she added.

The very same bedroom, next to the bathroom, where my own son Nathan now slept.

She also said areas of the house were distinctly cold, even in the summer… something we had also noted.

"It spooked me so much I couldn't go on living there, even though I loved everything else about the place," she added.

Just like Gill and I, this lady thought she was going crazy or imagining things. But we now knew we were not alone and we were far from crazy.

The lady asked me to report back to her on any more developments.

I later told Gill of my meeting at the Heritage Centre and we both spent the evening discussing our increasing incredulity about how events were now unfolding. And my God, they certainly were starting to unfold!

Chapter Eight
It's all Latin to Me

"Mysteries once thought to be supernatural or paranormal happenings - such as astronomical or meteorological events - are incorporated into science once their causes are understood."
Michael Shermer

Our lives now seemed to be skipping between the supernatural of ghosts, the surrealism of dreams and the reality of an undated burial ground lying under or adjacent to our house.

And the skipping was not about to stop… at least not yet.

During the night of Wednesday 15th January, just hours after my discussions at the Heritage Centre, another odd dream unfolded itself to me.

In this edge of darkness mind game there was a horse in our house and it kept rearing up on its hind legs to cuddle me. I was comforted in the dream by my wife telling me that: *"horses are affectionate pets and enjoy cuddles."*

Once again the dream remained vivid and life-like.

We laughed about it in the morning with Gill taunting me: *"People would pay to be in your dreams Nic!"*

But as sure as night follows day, our story was about to take another strange twist.

It was just after lunch the next day (Thursday 16th January) that I first spoke by telephone with a local history and archaeology expert and antiquarian book dealer called Mary Perry. I had been given her phone number by the lady at the Heritage Centre.

Mary was intrigued about the skeleton find… especially as she had never heard any information about it before. But she was even more deeply intrigued because her grandmother used to live in our cottage!

She said that there used to be a courtyard where our kitchen now stood. From her description it appears that our back living room had been the kitchen and scullery with a cooking range where our wood burning stove now sat.

The wood burning stove in the living room, which was once the site of the kitchen cooking range

And there had been an alley pathway at the side of the house into a courtyard where her gran did the washing and mangle dried the clothes. Beyond the courtyard there was a rose garden and rockeries.

Her grandmother eventually moved away from Plympton Cottage in 1938 and Mary said that as far as she knew: *"No human skeletons had been unearthed prior to that date."*

The garden of Plympton Cottage where the bones of a shire horse were buried – notice the raised level of the back of the garden

That means that the discovery of the skeletons must have taken place sometime between 1938 and 1950. And as six of those years were during World War II, the discovery was in all likelihood sometime between 1946 and 1950.

We felt that at last we had a breakthrough.

But it was what Mary told me next was to really shake me.

She recalled her grandmother telling her that during the 1930s the bones of a shire horse were unearthed from the end of our back garden.

After a few enquiries her grandmother discovered the horse had been buried prior to 1901 by the people who owned the old rectory to the rear of the property - behind where the new Sainsbury's supermarket now stands.

Clearly this was no obvious link to the buried human skeletons, but another haunting appendage to a dream and probably a link to the neighbouring stables built over 200 years earlier by the then rector Rev Francis Henry Egerton.

On Friday 17th January 2014 I mentioned the skeleton discovery to the husband of another former occupant of our house. He was deeply curious and wanted to know more before saying: *"You don't think you are haunted, do you?"*

I hadn't even mentioned the unexplained events or paranormal phenomena to him.

Then on Tuesday 21st January I tracked down yet another former occupant. The lady wished to remain anonymous as she too feared people would think she was crazy.

She said: *"I only stayed for six months. The cottage was lovely but it spooked me completely.*

"Things were always falling and there was a clanking sound downstairs at night. My dog would suddenly bark at shadows in the kitchen and I never felt I was alone… it was like someone was watching me all the time."

Over the following few days, four more people admitted to us personally of experiencing what most described as *"hauntings"* or *"strange things happening"* in our home.

Then as the final stages of this book were being completed in the autumn of 2019, Shropshire Council advisor Kelly Ford Evanson contacted me through social media to say: *"I also used to live there, myself and a few others experienced strange goings on in the house whilst being there."*

Su Broster, who lived in cottage in the 1980s and 1990s, said: *"There was always a smell of fish in the bedroom next to the bathroom, we searched to see where the smell was coming from and even took out the core of the fireplace to see if there anything behind it.*

"There was a strange feeling about the whole house, things were sometimes in different places in the kitchen and I would avoid going downstairs at night. I always had a feeling that something wasn't right with the place, which since we moved out I've not felt again.

"My son Aaron also remembers his cup of tea never being in the place he left it."

Su's sister Sharon Davies added that her own daughter Lauren recalls that often it felt like *"something"* knocked food out of her hands in the kitchen.

Spiritual Medium Jo Elson observed: *"The smell of fish is often linked to negative spirits, as is sulphur, like rotten eggs."*

Another former resident Nicola Williams said: *"We lived at Plympton Cottage between April 2002 and 2006. We had three daughters, a dog and two cats living there and did quite a lot of work on the house during that time, including blocking up the passageway from the kitchen to the front of the house and knocking through from the living room to the dining room and dry lining the kitchen wall.*

"We obviously had searches done etc when we purchased the house from Reeds Rains but nothing was ever mentioned.

"Also I was born in 1970 and grew up on Chester Road and have no recollection of anything ever having been mentioned about skeletons being found."

Fellow Whitchurch resident Pauline Jones added a different dimension and said: *"I lived the first 16 years of my life in Claypit Street (close to the old workhouse and hospital) and used to wander across the fields as a child.*

"The house I lived in definitely had a presence which I felt strongly as a child. My mother acknowledged and confided in her later life that she felt a presence too.

"I remember being told that there were ancient tunnels linking the area where Sainsbury's now stands to the old St Alkmund's Church. These tunnels would have run close to your cottage."

Everything about Plympton Cottage was now wrapped in intrigue and unanswered questions.

We felt an urge to dig deeper for evidence of both the skeletons and the paranormal activity in our home.

I found one online article entitled ***How Do I Know if my House is Haunted?*** really invaluable. It takes a balanced and logical approach to the subject and the writer gives the following advice:

Do You Have A Ghost In Your House? Or Other Paranormal Activity Going On?

One thing you may find if you have real paranormal activity going on in your home is cold spots. Is there a location in your home that is unusually cold?

The first thing to do is to conduct a thorough investigation. Always rule out the logical answers for unusual or unexplained activity first.

If possible buy a simple thermometer to take the temperature of your cold spot or cold spots.

Keep a journal and document what you find.

Snap Photos Often with a Digital Camera

Take photos with a digital camera around your house. If you suspect or think you have paranormal activity going on in a particular room or area take lots of photos in that area. And do it at different times of the day and night.

If you hear a strange noise take a photo in the direction of the noise. Then go through your photos carefully and look for people that were not there when the photo was taken or orbs or other lights.

If you spot something on a photo don't take it for proof of a ghost or paranormal activity, until you have examined the photo carefully and ruled out any logical solutions for anything strange in your photos.

Do You Have Objects That Move On Their Own?

Do you have a chair or other object that moves on its own?

Do you have a door or cabinet doors that you know for a fact you shut but they are open when you go back then you may indeed have something strange going on.

If possible set up a motion activated camera to see if you can catch the object moving.

If this is not possible be double sure you check the item out and go at once to it when you come back home or back into the area and you will know if something has moved. Again make double sure to look for logical solutions.

Do You Think Your House Is Haunted?

If it's possible and you think you have paranormal activity going on or you think your house is haunted thoroughly investigate the history of your home and the surrounding area.

Find out if there are deaths or tragic activity that are associated with your house or other location you suspect is haunted.

If you find out there was a death or several deaths of people who lived in your house then you may indeed have a haunted house or live in a house that has paranormal activity going on.

Be sure to keep a journal of everything going on around you. Write it down and document what is happening along with the date and time of what you see or hear.

Does it happen the same time every day? Then you may very well have a residual haunting going on.

Be sure to learn everything you can about the history of your house. You may be quite shocked at what you find out.

What to do if you see a Ghost

If you see a ghost try to have a camera handy and try to take its photo. Ask other family members or other people who live or have lived in your house what they have seen.

Don't tell them your full story of what you saw until they tell you their story. If their story matches up with what you saw then yes you may have a real haunting.

And again always keep a journal of what you are seeing along with the date and time. The more you can document the better off you will be.

Are these orbs in the Drop Spirit Zone?

Wonderful advice… and yes, we did have cold spots and cold areas, chairs and other objects did move on their own, our house did have a history of deaths and buried bodies, and previous residents corroborated the feeling that the cottage was haunted.

So after reading this I decided to take a series of about 20 photos in the *Drop Spirit Zone* in our kitchen. One particular picture rocked me. It appears to show more than half a dozen orbs or faint balls of light floating in that area of the kitchen. The lens of the camera was clean and the images only appear in one frame… all the other pictures I took remained clear.

What the hell was happening?

Then we skipped again and something weird and fascinating happened.

For as long as I have known I sometimes talk in my sleep.

On the night of Saturday 1st February (my 58th birthday) I had drunk a few glasses of wine and slept very deeply.

But not as deeply as I imagined.

Around 4am, Gill was woken by me muttering words and phrases in Latin. She used her iPhone to record my ramblings which included disturbing words such as *spiritu sancti* (holy spirit or holy ghost) and *malum* (evil). When I woke around 8am with vague memories of a dream I had the words *Dominy miseree nobise* rattling round my skull.

Gill couldn't wait to play me her recording.

We sat there in bed and talked at length about my dream, my sleep talking and in particular the words I awoke to.

Together we looked them up on the internet and those waking words appear to be Latin for *Domine Miserere Nobis*, which translated means: *Lord Have Mercy Upon Us*.

I must make clear that I have absolutely no knowledge of Latin, and for the one year I studied the subject at grammar school, some 45 years earlier, I never got further than declining the verbs Amo, Amas, Amat. I was forced to drop Latin at the end of my first year after finishing 32nd out of 32 pupils in the class.

So the mysteries of the dreams remained and worse than that I was now reciting Latin in my sleep!

Chapter Nine
Roman Holiday

"If you have a garden and a library, you have everything you need."
Marcus Tullius Cicero

In order to get some answers to our questions it became clear that we had to deal with things that were tangible and for which there may be real physical evidence.

Or at least, as my late father would have said: *"You have to apply logic... test every theory you might have."*

So we had to try and find the real origins of the skeletons which we now believed had been unearthed from the grounds of our cottage sometime in the late 1940s.

Could they really be Roman, as the first excavation report suggested or from another era entirely? As mentioned earlier, Whitchurch is the only town in Shropshire on an original Roman site.

A selection of Roman burial vases are on display at the Civic Centre. These were excavated during refurbishments at 33 High Street (where the *Docket No. 33* restaurant now stands) in the early 1980s, and they led archaeological experts to believe that this was part of a formal enclosed Roman burial site below the fort at the top of the High Street. This site lies at least 600 yards south of our cottage and well beyond the crest of the hill where St Alkmund's Church stands.

But a larger Roman cremation cemetery is believed to have existed in Doddington, on the other side of town, after a succession of Roman cremation urns and burial artefacts were found in the same locality.

Many of these discoveries were made when the new housing estate at Queensway next to Sedgeford was being developed more than 40 years ago. They confirmed earlier archaeological views of Roman burials formed between 1899 and the 1970s.

Six cremations were found at Sedgeford in 1973. One cremation pit contained a ring-necked flagon, over 100 iron nails and a bronze mirror. These finds dated to the mid 2nd century AD and the cemetery to the 1st and 2nd century AD.

The fields behind Queensway in Doddington where the Roman cremation cemeteries were discovered

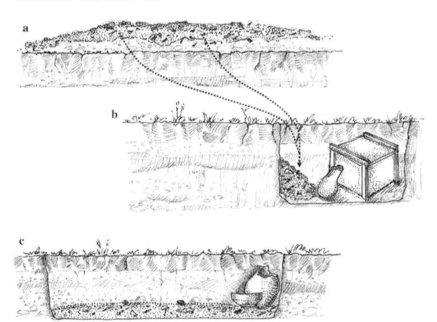

Details of a Roman cremation grave

During a further phase of work on the housing development at Queensway in 1975 a further eight cremation burials were recorded.

All were dug into natural sand and lay directly below topsoil and garden cultivation.

The Romans first built a fort in the heart of the town, which has been tentatively suggested as forming part of the border defences, established by Ostorius Scapula around AD 52. By about AD 100, however, the Roman army had probably moved on and the surrounding indigenous civilian population would have taken over the site.

In the mid 2nd century AD, the area was at least partly covered by timber-framed industrial buildings. The town reached the height of its prosperity by the early 3rd century and there was much rebuilding in stone.

In 2016 – a year after we left Whitchurch - archaeologists discovered more remains of Roman civilisation during work on a culvert south of the London Road.

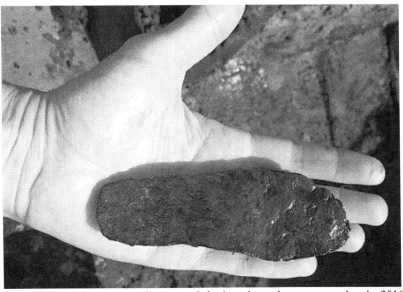

A Roman child's shoe as discovered during the culvert excavation in 2016

The remains were discovered by archaeologists from Shropshire Council's historic environment team and Salford University, during excavation work by the Environment Agency.

65

The site lies on the northern edge of the town centre, just beyond the likely edge of the Roman settlement and about 400 yards from Plympton Cottage.

Before the project began it was identified that the line of the culvert to the south of London Road had some potential to contain historic remains. As a result, archaeologists from the Centre for Applied Archaeology at Salford University were on hand when work for the new culvert began.

However, the archaeologists were surprised to discover an unexpectedly rich series of waterlogged deposits that included the remains of a wooden trackway, a number of structural timbers, a large amount of Roman pottery and, most importantly of all, 15 leather shoes.

Both adult and children's shoes were present, a number of which were complete and included fine Roman impressed decorations.

The finds that were recovered during the construction of the new culvert were preserved by the wet silts along the side of the brook.

Work remains ongoing but archaeologists think that the trackway lay immediately beyond the edge of the Roman town and crossed the wet valley bottom. The other finds appear to result from the dumping of rubbish along the edge of an open stream.

Whilst the archaeological finds gave a new insight into Roman life in the town there was no indication of any further Roman burial site.

Indeed the earlier archaeological discoveries both at Queensway and the 2016 ones at the culvert off the London Road are very important, because they date the primary Roman occupation of Whitchurch as 1st and 2nd century AD.

Because although inhumation (burial of bodies) was practised regularly in ancient archaic Rome, cremation was the most common burial practice in the mid to late Republic and the Empire well into the 1st and 2nd centuries. As the finds at Queensway testify.

Cremation was one of the primary forms of burial for Roman period until the rise of Christianity in the 3rd century AD. Funeral rites took place at home and at the place of burial, which was located outside the town or city walls to avoid the pollution of the living.

So although any Roman origin for the Plympton Cottage skeletons is impossible to prove with any certainty, in light of the above facts that origin now seems highly unlikely.

So were the skeletons from a later period in the so-called Dark Ages or early Middle Ages, between the 7th and 13th centuries when a moated monastery appeared to have stood on the site of the old rectory?

As previously mentioned, the name Whitchurch is from the Middle English for White Church, referring to a church constructed of white stone in the Norman period. The area was also known as Album Monasterium and the land owning Warennes family of Whitchurch were often surnamed de Albo Monasterio in contemporary writings.

William fitz Ranulf is the earliest individual of the Warenne family recorded as the Lord of Whitchurch, Shropshire, first appearing in the Shropshire Pipe Roll of 1176.

But no written first hand evidence exists of the monastery – its actuality is only formed by vague archaeological finds – and certainly no burial records. Therefore to ascribe the burials at Plympton Cottage to either Roman or Saxon monastic origin is purely conjecture or educated guesswork.

But there were other hypotheses to unravel and two in particular added something more credible to our mystery.

And these other alternatives are also truly fascinating.

Chapter Ten
Plague

"You must picture the consternation of our little town, hitherto so tranquil, and now, out of the blue, shaken to its core, like a quite healthy man who all of a sudden feels his temperature shoot up and the blood seething like wildfire in his veins."
Albert Camus

I have already mentioned the Black Death earlier in this book… and here is where the world's most devastating pestilence returns home in this narrative.

Black Death is the name given to three types of Plague that were common in Europe during the middle of the 14th Century: Bubonic Plague was caused a swelling of the glands. It was believed to have been spread by fleas from rats. Pneumonic Plague affected people's lungs, causing them to cough up blood. It is thought to have been spread by people breathing or coughing on one another. Septicaemic Plague was rarer and went straight into the bloodstream of its victims, killing them quickly.

One of the most visible side effects of the disease was red spots covering the entire body. These spots turned black and then victims would almost certainly die. Hence the name Black Death.

As mentioned earlier in this book, the disease first arrived in England on the south coast via a trade boat in the summer of 1348. It spread across the south in bubonic form during those summer months before mutating into the even more frightening pneumonic form with the onset of winter. It hit London in September 1348 and spread into East Anglia and all along the east coast early the New Year. By spring 1349, it had reached Shropshire and rapidly spread around the county.

The clergy were unable to keep up with demands to perform services for the dying and often became the dead themselves. Widespread panic must have existed with unaffected people wondering whether they would be next. It is likely that Shropshire's death toll would have been much greater if it had not been so rural.

Bodies of Plague victims were sometimes buried in communal Plague pits dug outside the town walls. Where this occurred, the bodies were dumped naked on top of each other before being covered in earth and lime.

A brass engraving of John le Strange and his wife Anakretta le Botiler in London – both died of the Black Death

Records show that independently wealthy John le Strange who owned the manor house just east of Plympton Cottage (which was later rebuilt as the rectory) died of the Black Death on 20th August 1349, with the inquest into his death scheduled to take place on 30th August. Two days before the inquest, however, John's eldest son Fulk also fell victim to Plague, as well as his younger brother Humphrey.

This left John's youngest son John to inherit the three water mills and all the Le Strange land, but his land was deemed worthless because all its tenants and domestic servants were dead and *"no-one is willing to hire the land"*.

Evidence from court rolls confirms that the Plague was at its height during the summer and autumn. At Kinnerley (west of Shrewsbury) 14 tenements, amounting to a quarter of the customary land, were vacant by Michaelmas and at Prees (south of Whitchurch) there were 22 vacant holdings.

The Black Death generated a much higher level of mortality than usual among the gentry and many great families were suddenly shaken and their security threatened, their wealth and social status undermined.

The le Strange family was exceptionally unlucky in losing male family members during three successive outbreaks of the Plague - two in 1349, and one each in 1361 and 1375. By 1375 not even the relative fecundity of the family in producing sons for the next generation could help them escape extinction in the male line.

Anakretta le Botiler survived her husband, John le Strange, until the next visitation of the Plague in 1361. And it broke out again between 1362-62 and then again in 1368-69, 1371-75 and continued into the 15th century. Death rates were lower than during the Black Death but the new outbreaks seemed to affect younger people more. Modern research shows that it was possible for the Plague bacteria to have become both age and gender specific by the 1360s. And by the 1370s the population or England had halved, so there was a dire need to bury the corpses anywhere and by anyone.

The inquisition post mortem record on the death of John le Strange

Indeed, records show that all of John le Strange's tenants at his manor at Broughton, 27 miles away on the Welsh borders, died from the Black Death and were buried on the estate.

But as a wealthy member of the gentry and an owner of the land where Plympton Cottage would later be built, there is a strong probability that the le Strange victims of the Black Death would have been buried on their own land. And because of their status, they may have been afforded a proper Christian burial with prayers and Latin psalms and interred in graves on their own land together with their staff and servants rather than having their bodies dumped in a common grave. After all, their estate was well away from the town's Roman walls and the wider population.

Dr Hugh Wilmott from Sheffield University's department of archaeology who oversaw the excavation in 2016 of a mass Black Death burial ground in Lincolnshire containing 48 skeletons, observed in a report in the **Independent** newspaper: *"Despite that fact it is now estimated that up to half the population of England perished during the Black Death, multiple graves associated with the event are extremely rare in this country, and it seems local communities continued to dispose of their loved ones in as ordinary way as possible."*

The Plague was almost endemic in medieval England and Whitchurch was again hit by the disease during the 17th century in the same way that London suffered in 1665.

London Plagues were not widespread around the country in the 17th century but Whitchurch had been involved in a few outbreaks since the first one in 1625. The churchwardens' accounts for that year recorded prayers that the Plague might be stayed and a few months later recorded thanksgiving when the death toll lessened.

However, as the parish registers do not officially begin until 1630, the effect of this epidemic on the population of the town cannot be determined.

But 12 years later in 1642 there were 137 burials and nearly the half of these were in the autumn months of September, October and November. It is possible that Plague was, at least in part, the cause of the increased number deaths.

Parish records reveal that the first epidemic to hit Whitchurch in 1648-1649 was possibly an outbreak of Typhus Fever – records show a spike of more than 20 burials a month in 1648 peaking at 42 burials in September. But by the summer of 1649 burials had fallen to less than 10 a month. And interestingly none of these were noted as *"Plague burials"*.

An etching showing the disposal of bodies into a 17th century Plague pit

A bigger epidemic mainly in 1650 but continuing into 1651 was specifically named as *Plague* in the parish register, and the names of those believed to have died from the Plague were marked with a cross. Though the term Plague could simply mean any form of pestilence, in a town such as Whitchurch where outbreaks of the Plague had occurred previously, the symptoms of bubonic Plague were distressingly obvious and familiar.

In this year 119 died from the Plague: 23 men, 32 women, 57 boys and girls and seven small children. Of the 184 burials in 1650, 111 (60%) were attributed to "Plague".

The real outbreak began in August 1650 and the last recorded death was in May the following year, but the bulk of the deaths, 95 (80%), occurred in August, September and October 1650, the worst month being September with 42 deaths.

In the winter of 1650/51 the Plague was still present, but monthly burials were in single figures.

However, this epidemic showed strong familial incidences. The 119 deaths involved 60 families and in only 21 of these did a single member die, so it seems that quarantining infected households may have stopped the Plague spreading further. The most acutely affected families were those of John and Mary Wright with four of their children, and William and Mary Ranshall and five of their children. In a further six families the husband and children died, including Thomas Cowper and five children.

A further characteristic of this Plague epidemic was its strongly localised nature. The churchwardens' accounts include Christ-tide lists of the parishioners and from these the residence of about three-quarters of those mentioned in the burial register for 1642 can be traced, and about half of these were in the centre of the town, a proportion reflecting the balance of the population.

In 1649 again the residence of about half of those dying could be traced, and rather more, about two-thirds, had lived in the town. Of the Plague deaths in 1650 the place of residence of half could be traced, but only three people lived in the hamlets, and one of those was a churchwarden who would have had to come into the town.

The Plague victims whose residence is known appear to have almost all lived in the High Street from the top of Bargates (which was also the market) and a small lane known as Pepper Street leading off the High Street, where the outbreak began and where the last Plague death was recorded. Historians believe all of these would have been buried in a communal Plague pit, whose location is unknown.

As in the 14th century outbreaks, bodies of the Plague victims were still usually buried in pits dug outside the town walls and by now well away from water supplies.

But unlike the Black Death outbreaks of mediaeval times, it seems the bodies were not simply dumped naked on top of each other before being covered in earth and lime (where available), but wherever possible they were afforded a Christian burial and interred in an extended state.

During recent excavations for the 73 miles of Crossrail tracks and tunnels in London a Plague pit from 1665 was unearthed beside Liverpool Street Station where 4,000 skeletons were discovered with remnants of coffin wood.

Jay Carver, the head archaeologist on the Crossrail site, told the *Independent* newspaper: *"There are many examples of head-to-toe burials, apparently adopted due to a real lack of space, but mostly head west, east feet."*

And unlike medieval Plague pits, the Crossrail bodies were coffined even when space didn't allow in an east-west alignment. Carver said: *"It seems that even at this time of crisis, people were making considerable efforts to give their dead a decent Christian burial."*

So again one can surmise that the skeletons at Plympton Cottage may quite possibly be a Plague graveyard – although whether these are from the 1349 Black Death outbreak, which took the wealthy le Strange family, or from the 1650 outbreak where families often died and were then buried together, there is no way of really knowing, without further excavation work and proper scientific Carbon 14 dating of the skeletons.

Chapter Eleven
Ley Lines and Gentry

"Philanthropy is commendable, but it must not cause the philanthropist to overlook the circumstances of economic injustice which make philanthropy necessary."
Martin Luther King

Alfred Watkins's key academic text book:
The Old Straight Track

Interestingly the town of Whitchurch lies on a *'significant'* ancient ley-line.

Alfred Watkins (1855–1935) the author of the controversial academic text ***The Old Straight Track*** originated the idea of ley-lines and surveyed alignments which articulated the prehistoric landscape of Britain, in his native Herefordshire in the 1920s.

Despite the scepticism of some academic archaeologists, his vision of ley-lines (invisible lines that connected prehistoric sites across England) helped shape popular views of the British landscape.

Watkins argued that ley-lines were alignments of places of geographical or historical interest such as ancient monuments, megaliths, natural ridge tops and fords. He believed that in ancient times, when Britain was far more densely forested, the country was crisscrossed by a network of straight-line travel routes, with prominent features of the landscape being used as navigation points.

In 1936, the idea was put forward that ley-lines were lines of power, linking prehistoric sites, although what sorts of powers might be involved were not specified. The scene was thus set for the elevation of ancient trackways to something more spiritual.

A website on **Earth's Grid Systems** describes several features that may be responsible for the phenomenon known as ley-lines.

One of these so-called *Hartmann Lines* consists of naturally occurring electrically charged lines, running North-South and East-West to form a grid system across the Earth's surface with a distance of about 2 metres in the north-south direction and 2.5 metres in the east-west direction.

Alternate lines are usually positively and negatively charged, so where the lines intersect it is possible to have double positive charges and double negative charges, or one positive and one negative charge. It is the intersections that are seen by some experts to be a source of potential paranormal problems and spiritual energy.

Ley-lines are also connected geographically with all manner of enigmatic lines in the landscape, such as dowsing lines, feng shui and the patterns scraped on the remote Nazca plateau of Peru which are claimed to evoke the *"spirits of the dead"*.

So could these *Hartmann Lines* point to geological and electrical reasons for hauntings in a place such as Whitchurch? Or is the reason something more specific to a particular building or place?

A similar electrically charged **Stone Tape Theory (STT)** is frequently used as a scientific explanation of hauntings and ghostly activity. Paranormal investigators use the idea to account for appearances of images, sounds, and apparitions that do not interact directly with people. Instead, they play out like a movie or recording. This is most commonly termed *'residual haunting'* to suggest something was left behind in the past to account for the current effects perceived.

The premise of *STT* is that crystalline rock (bedrock or building stone) captured emotional energy from a traumatic event. The preferred rock type is said to be quartz but limestone is mentioned as frequently.

The sound and visual representations of an event are recorded into the fabric of the rock media in a process analogous to a magnetic VHS tape recording of data.

At a much later date, a person sensitive to this energy can receive the playback or the playback can be initiated by certain conditions. The recording/playback sequence has long been used as an explanation for apparition sightings and haunting.

The mechanisms proposed for the environmental recording/playback loop include invisible energy fields, molecular architecture of crystalline quartz, energy fields from dead organisms that make up limestone, resonant frequencies, encoded of iron oxide crystals, inductive electromagnetism, and quantum entanglement.

But what of the probable history of the land immediately surrounding Plympton Cottage?

Exhaustive research at Shropshire County library in Whitchurch began to unravel some strands of the mystery.

And all our deskbound findings appeared to centre on the old rectory which stood on a site some 200 yards due east of the cottage.

As recently as 1900 the rectory lands extended further east to incorporate the old workhouse and west to include our cottage, the adjoining Bargates House and the gardens of The Gables.

It is important to understand something of the nature of this area of land.

The Domesday Book of 1086 notes the aforementioned early Saxon monastery at the Westune (Whitchurch) settlement which was surrounded by a moat... this is the site on which the le Strange manor would be built upon.

The origins of the moated site are obscure. It was once thought that a medieval hospital dependant on Haughmond Abbey was founded here for the poor, aged and infirm in the 13th century.

Little is known about this old le Strange building in the 15th and 16th centuries, but a church *Terrier and Inventory* dated 14th October 1612 described a 'Parsonage House' of seven bays all within the moat, and outside the moat were a kiln of two bays and a seven bayed barn. Later, an inventory of the rector Matthew Fowler (1666-1683) gives an image of the house in the later 17th century. He had six bedchambers, a great and little parlour, a hall, a kitchen as well as a coach house and stables for four horses.

The wealthy and flamboyant Rev Francis Henry Egerton

In about 1600 the whole site passed into the ownership of Sir Thomas Egerton, the Lord Chancellor. By 1612 the former moated manor had become the *Rectory House*, apparently descending together throughout the medieval and post medieval periods.

In 1749 the rector obtained permission to demolish the existing manor house sitting within 35 acres of land and replace it with a new one. The replacement rectory built of red brick and slate lay on the east side of the moated area, clear of the site of the old building. The whole of the moat interior west of the new house was given over to a pleasure garden, including a walled court or terrace containing the turning circle and with a projection to the west.

The remains of the old Egerton rectory as it stands today

In 1781 the rectory of Whitchurch was taken over by the wealthy and flamboyant Francis Henry Egerton. Three years later he commissioned famed 18th century architect William Emes to suggest improvements to the rectory and its lands.

His plan appears to be typical of the landscaping of that period with the use of winding pathways and drives; belts of trees to screen areas such as the stables, farmyard and ice house and small copses in the wider landscape to provide more screening. The servants' quarters to the rectory adjoined the main house and were

79

comprehensive to include a kitchen, a servants' hall, a pantry, a scullery with a large meat and game larder and a coal house outside.

The underground Ice House (where meat and other perishable food could be stored) survives and is a historical focal point in the new Sainsbury's supermarket car park. There was also stabling for three horses with hay-lofts, a saddle room and a coach house.

The Ice House, now a feature of the Sainsbury's car park

A plan made seven years later in 1791 appears to show that the main drive to the rectory enters from Claypit Street; but there is no indication that a planned driveway from Bargates - alongside Plympton Cottage - was ever constructed, although a path is indicated leading from the rectory to St Alkmund's Church. There is also an indication of a small cemetery beyond the Ice House.

However a 1797 lithograph does give a semblance of life to these plans. Among images of animal housing and a man hard at work, the main house in the etching looks very much like Bargates House with a small cottage attached to it (the original hovel where Plympton Cottage would later be extended) and in the distance can be seen the unmistakable tower of the recently built St Alkmund's Church.

A 1797 lithograph appears to show **Bargates House and Plympton Cottage**, with the tower of St Alkmund's Church visible to the right

A much later detailed town plan of 1879 shows the rectory gardens in great detail and it is of particular interest to Plympton Cottage. The kitchen gardens were still in use at that period and two greenhouses are visible.

To the north lies a pump and trough. There are formal divisions within the garden and there is a footbridge across the moat. Just to the east of the site boundary is a summer house.

But it is to the west of the rectory where our interest lies. Beyond another Summer House and stepped formal gardens the rectory lands extend to Tarporley Road and include Bargates House and a very different looking plan of the adjoining Plympton Cottage. The cottage itself has a water cistern attached to its northern wall, extends to the road edge to the west and has a truncated boundary to the west and large gardens to the rear.

But of even greater interest is that within the large and conjoined extended formal gardens – bordered by a gated track and trees – the land where The Gables now stands is vacant.

But just beyond that is a complex of at least 12 stables, huts, small cottages and agricultural and horticultural buildings – almost like a small stand-alone community within the rectory lands, well away from the rectory itself.

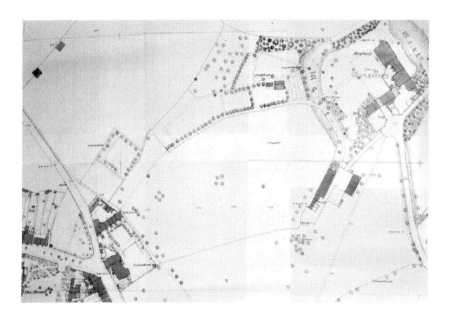

The 1897 plan of the rectory estate shows in the bottom left Plympton
Cottage and neighbouring property, including other buildings and hovels.
Below a more recent plan shows the same area of land and The Gables
house which replaced the agricultural buildings.

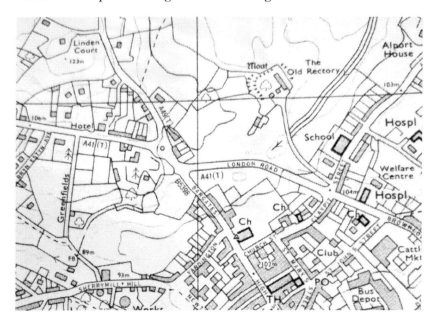

82

For 50 years (1779-1829) the rectory was home to Whitchurch's most eccentric and beneficent rector, the Rev Francis Henry Egerton, younger son of John Egerton, the Bishop of Durham.

Francis became rector of Whitchurch in 1781 when he was just 25 years old. Educated at Eton and Christ Church Oxford he was a man of many talents and great wealth. He was a noted British eccentric from the Egerton family and a supporter of natural theology. Egerton kept dogs and cats in his house which he dressed as ladies and gentlemen and would take them with him in his carriage in London and Paris.

He never married, but reputedly had five illegitimate children, including at least one daughter and two more in Paris.

But despite his wayward and eccentric manner, this man may yet provide the key to our research.

Chapter Twelve
Work your way to the Grave

"It is death that goes down to the centre of the earth, the great burial church the earth is, and then to the curved ends of the universe, as light is said to do."
Harold Brodkey

The socially conscious Rev Francis Henry Egerton was interested in plans for a new workhouse to be built at Deermoss, a few hundred yards to the west of the rectory. This would replace the old *House of Industry* in the Newtown area on the western edge of Whitchurch, which was deemed no longer fit for use and condemned by a government inspection.

In 1791 the old workhouse was described as consisting of two small houses joined together by a third building which housed 60 men, women and children.

So plans for a new brick built workhouse were drawn up and building work began immediately.

By 1794 Francis Henry Egerton's new imposing Union Workhouse was constructed on a high undeveloped site adjacent to Claypit Street, with initial accommodation for up to 40 inmates. The design included workrooms, a schoolroom, two wards for the sick and a mortuary.

It was maintained with money collected from the Poor Rate payable by householders in the Parish according to the value of their property (a fiscal ancestor of 20th century rates). This was testimony to pioneering social welfare provision in the Whitchurch and in many ways anticipated the national reform of poor law operations instituted in 1834, which required all parishes to provide provisions for the poor.

Francis Henry Egerton had a generous side to his character. He concerned himself greatly with the plight of the poor and often acted politically against other neighbouring landowners and deputies who tried to enact more punitive and callous acts against poor people.

He also showed a paternal grace to many of the inmates of the workhouse and found work for them in the rectory grounds as gardeners, stable hands, agricultural labourers and water carriers.

With these jobs came convenient accommodation in small cottages or hovels alongside Tarporley Road some 500 yards west of the actual workhouse.

Francis Henry Egerton's related successor William Henry Egerton (1811-1910) became the new rector on 20th February 1846.

Whitchurch's Local Act status made it immune from many of the provisions of the 1834 Poor Law Amendment Act. However, in 1854, a new Whitchurch Poor Law Union was created which took in inmates in parishes from Nantwich and other adjacent Unions.

The population falling within the union at the 1851 census had been 11,400 with parishes ranging in size from Chidlow (population 12) to Whitchurch town itself (5,976).

Also a wealthy man, William Henry Egerton lived the life of a country gentleman and although not as eccentric as his predecessor he was also a philanthropist, helping the poor at various regular intervals. Under his stewardship the new Union Workhouse was substantially enlarged in 1853.

It became a symmetrical red-brick building facing to the south-east. Women and children were housed in the eastern part of the building and men in the western part. An infirmary block was added at the north. A casual ward block, complete with sleeping and work cells, stood at the western corner of the site.

In 1861, the Poor Law Board published a return of the name of every adult pauper who had been a workhouse inmate for a continuous period of five years or more, together with the duration of their residence (in years and months).

Many people came and went from the workhouse, but a contemporary report from the 1861 census lists eight long-term inmates: John Barrow, classified as lame there for seven years; Peter Alcock there for seven years; Thomas Brett, classified as *'old age'* had been in the workhouse for 11 years, a similarly classified John Whittingham for six years; John Benion classified as *'lame and an idiot'* for six years; Mary Penkey who was *'lame'* had been an inmate for six years; Mary Venables had been incarcerated for 20 years and finally Ann Hayward who had been in the workhouse for 14 years and was cruelly classified as an '*imbecile*'.

The Union workhouse as it looked in the later 19th century

But more interesting to us was the census report for 1881 showing both the 10 staff and the 101 inmates at the workhouse. These include a 70-year-old old inmate named Mary Purcell – with no record of her husband – and the family of former farmer John Venables aged 77, his wife and former charwoman Martha Venables aged 70, and a 16-year-old Harriet Venables – possibly their grand-daughter?

Although people with these surnames had populated my dreams and may have worked in the neighbouring stable block, there is nothing verifiable to show they were buried in the grounds of Plympton Cottage when they died.

This is especially doubtful given that the 1879 map of the rectory estate shows the already mentioned small formal graveyard some 400 yards west of our cottage - and closer to the workhouse – now adjacent to where the vehicular entrance to the Sainsbury's car park stands.

More than half the main workhouse building was demolished and most of the out-buildings, including the former infirmary block in the early 20th century.

Deermoss Hospital in the early 20ᵗʰ century

Part of the building was converted into Deermoss Hospital for use by the general population after the end of the Poor Law in the 1930s. Now all that remains on the site as a reminder of the workhouse is the small Victorian red brick cottage hospital, which also provides some geriatric care.

Once again had my dreams come back to bite me?

Jim Hewitson observes in his book **Dead Weird**: *"Death is simply much more than shutting down of a life system or even a soul taking flight. It is as much about those left behind as it is about the deceased – perhaps more. The cords that bind us stretch beyond death and are strong."*

He goes on to say: *"One curious superstition related to death is a belief that the spirit of the last person buried in a certain place keeps watch among the living until the next burial."*

Chapter Thirteen
Exodus

"All my bags are packed
I'm ready to go
I'm standin' here outside your door
I hate to wake you up to say goodbye"
John Denver

In November 2014, due to job changes, combined with our tenants wishing to vacate our house in Wolverhampton, we made the reluctant decision to terminate our own tenancy of Plympton Cottage.

Despite – or maybe because of – all the intrigue surrounding ghosts and skeletons, we actually loved living in the cottage. Anyway we soon began packing for yet another house move set for the end of January 2015.

During our last month living in the cottage we arranged our final investigation.

This time we invited a local spiritual medium and member of **Whitchurch Paranormal Society**, a fascinating lady named Jo Elson, to visit us.

She arrived at the cottage on a dark cold night in January and stayed for about 90 minutes, chatting and conducting a few simple experiments.

She could not sense any measurable paranormal activity.

Then, while she was standing and chatting to Gill and me in our kitchen inside the so-called *Drop Spirit Zone*, both she and I noticed a sudden spark of unknown energy shoot across the quarry-tiled floor and out through the living room door.

And that was that… whatever it was had gone.

"I have a sneaky feeling you have calmed things down by giving a voice to all the goings on," she later said.

We lit a candle and burned some sage and lavender, which was recommended by Jo to cleanse a haunted area.

But our journey was not done yet.

Shortly before we moved house I gained some clarity about the discovery of the skeletons.

While talking to an elderly neighbour I discovered that our kitchen extension was built at the same time as The Gables house to the north of our property.

It was during the building excavations for this house and our kitchen – which lies some four feet lower than the footings of the property next door – that our skeletons were unearthed.

The garden level of Plympton Cottage is higher than the excavated kitchen, which is also four feet lower than the land at The Gables next door

It was assumed by the builders who unearthed the skeletons in the 1940s that there were likely to be more buried in the same vicinity both in the gardens of our cottage and the large house next door.

I guess we may never know.

Then by a twist of fate, later that year archaeologists from Aeon Archaeology returned to dig two evaluation trenches just 40 yards away (GR SJ5398 4196) before construction of a new home was allowed at a property known as The Croft. The property lay attached to the other side of Bargates House (and was originally part of the same structure) on the junction of Tarporley Road and London Road at the northern edge of their *"postulated cemetery."*

A modern aerial photograph shows the relative locations of each of the properties

One excavated trench did identify some Roman features but these were interpreted as having a domestic function rather than being associated with the cemetery.

Aeon reported: *"The smaller trench to the south contained no archaeological remains, however the large trench which ran 30m by 4m across the proposed development yielded three features with an abundance of Roman potsherds, including rims. Evaluation of the features has shown that they are more likely to be associated with domestic activity and may be drainage gullies and discrete refuse pits which are common features in and around settlements."*

The Aeon archaeology trenches were dug well to the left of the child's swing. Plympton Cottage is on the far right of this photograph.

And to clarify, the archaeologists' report added: *"There are no known prehistoric archaeological sites or find-spots within the Site or in the vicinity, but during the Romano-British period Whitchurch was established as a Roman town. A cemetery to the north-western of the settlement is suspected and if present is likely to have been tightly focussed along Bargates and possibly along the roadside.*

"The suspicion derives from a report, dated to 1950, that seven skeletons were found in the grounds of the residential premises The Gables and Plympton,

91

c. 30m to the south-east of the Site's southern boundary. There appears to be no further information on the skeletons other than an annotation on a map made by an Ordnance Survey correspondent in 1950 and an Ordnance Survey Record Card dating to 1976.

The existence of further inhumations in the vicinity remains conjectural but there is a chance that the seven inhumations may be accompanied by more, as yet undiscovered human remains, and that if present such remains may extend into the Site."

So the new dig returned no evidence at all of a larger burial plot than that discovered decades earlier in the grounds of our old cottage.

When we moved away from Whitchurch in January 2015, we were left no wiser as to whether the skeletons had been removed and re-buried somewhere else or were simply covered with rubble and concrete by overly busy post war builders.

But right up until the date of our house move, we still experienced dozens of things falling in the *Drop Spirit Zone* – a box of six eggs sliding across the kitchen table and smashing to the floor, followed by a pack of bacon and two slices of bread were all quite memorable. It was like ghosts preparing breakfast and it was all part and parcel of living in that cottage.

We eventually moved house on Friday 30th January 2015.

But the spirits of Plympton Cottage had not finished yet.

Almost 10 months after moving away, on Wednesday, 11th November 2015, I drove to Whitchurch to spend the evening with an old friend.

We had arranged to meet at a local pub at 7pm but I arrived early in the town. I nipped into Sainsbury's to buy some beers for later in the evening before spontaneously deciding to park my car outside my former home and pay some last respects to Plympton Cottage.

I got out of the car to stretch my legs and looked at the front of the building.

Suddenly my mobile phone buzzed in my back pocket. I took the phone out to see if there was a text or email message for me. To my surprise the phone was frozen with only the time displaying on the lock screen.

I tried to unfreeze the phone, but with no luck. Even removing the SIM and memory cards failed to jog the phone back into life!

Two hours later with the phone still frozen, I explained my predicament to my friend as we supped a beer in the local pub.

Our final view of Plympton Cottage before we moved away from Whitchurch in January 2015

Together we finally managed a hard reset on the phone and brought it back to life… but I had sadly lost over 200 saved photographs, including many of the *Drop Spirit Zone*.

Then the penny dropped: were the spirits having a last laugh at me to let me know they were still there?

Who know!

But I have not been back… and those spirits probably still walk that twilight zone which we have yet to understand.

But for now this is my truth… this is the way I believe the world actually is.

Or as HP Lovecraft wrote: *"We may guess that in dreams life, matter, and vitality, as the earth knows such things, are not necessarily constant; and that time and space do not exist as our waking selves comprehend them."*

Afterword

A stone wall carving in St Alkmund's Church

As I wrote in the Foreword to this book, my story would probably leave you with more questions than answers.

- We have no definitive concrete proof of when the seven skeletons were buried under or near our kitchen, although we have a good provenance that they were discovered sometime between 1946 and 1950.
- We have no idea what became of the bones nor whether they are still interred in the ground.
- We cannot explain rationally any of my dreams or premonitions – they remain all part of HP Lovecraft's so-called unknown universe.
- We also cannot explain the many strange events which occurred during our time living in Plympton Cottage – nor the unexplained activity experienced by many others, including other previous residents.

The purpose of this book is to document the 18 months we lived in Plympton Cottage and not to persuade others to believe our shared truth. After all, not everyone believes in ghosts, spirits or the after-life.

But now, as I write this **Afterword**, I am absolutely certain that there is something paranormal in our world which we do not yet understand and cannot yet explain.

So, is it possible that an individual's identity or stream of consciousness continues after the death of the physical body? It is a hypothesis which has extended the thoughts of great minds for centuries.

Prof Sam Parnia

There are many different theories as to how the afterlife may play out and whether ghosts or spirits of the dead can exist.

UK scientist Professor Sam Parnia, who is director of the *Human Consciousness Project* at the University of Southampton, believes human consciousness does live on after we die.

Dr Parnia has studied more than 100 cases of cardiac arrest survivors. These are patients who technically died and came back to life, and Dr Parnia says a large percentage had bizarre experiences when they did.

"We know that actually for thousands of years, people who have come close to death for any reason have had these very profound, deep and in some ways mystical experiences," he explains.

"People feel an immense sense of peace, comfort and joy when they go through death.

"They may describe a sensation of actually meeting deceased relatives, friends, or others that they don't really know.

"So I think what we are beginning to understand is that we have very much a universal experience of death."

Dr Parnia explained how these first-hand accounts can be supported by science.

"It's important to understand that when a person is dying and they've turned into a cadaver, it's only at that point that the cells inside the body start to undergo a process of death, which can take hours, if not days," he says.

"So actually we have this window of time where we can bring people back to life and the experiences that they have given us is an indication of what it is like to go through death.

"Today we call the soul consciousness in science, so we can test the theory scientifically.

"The evidence we have is that when a person dies, that part that makes us who we are — the soul or mind, or whatever you call it — it does not become annihilated."

In 2014, Dr James Porter Morland, an American philosopher who currently serves as a professor at Talbot School of Theology at Biola University in California, declared that there is definitely an afterlife. He also claimed to have scientific evidence to support his views. *"I think there are certain pieces of evidence that there is certainly an afterlife,"* he said. *"The question of whether the mind or consciousness can exist outside the brain is not a scientific question. Let me dispute the claim that everything can be rooted in the brain, if that's true, there's no free will."*

Dr Morland took things one step further, claiming the brain does not store memories as a simple organic piece of body matter.

"That means that consciousness is an epiphenomenon, it's a by-product, it's caused by the brain, but it doesn't, in turn, cause anything. If that's true, then

the acceptance of scientific theories is determined by your brain chemistry," he said.

"The idea that memories are in the brain is absolutely gobbledygook – it makes no sense at all. Memories aren't the sort of thing that can be spatially located in a piece of chemistry."

But what about ghosts, poltergeists and spirits? Academics are now starting to devote serious research time into such supernatural occurrences.

There are currently more than 500 academic texts published in the UK on ghosts and poltergeists with a number of them focussing on electromagnetic field activity, as discussed briefly in Chapter 11 of this book.

One such academic paper titled ***Rationale and Application of a Multi-Energy Sensor Array in the Investigation of Haunting and Poltergeist Cases*** was first published by James Houran and Rense Lange in 1998.

An abstract from the paper states: *"Evidence from field studies and case analyses implicates electromagnetic field activity in processes underpinning hauntings and poltergeist-like episodes. Consistent with these findings, a comprehensive literature review shows that previous procedures often included indices of electromagnetic field activity.*

"Unfortunately, most of these approaches have been limited by the fact that variables of interest were collected and studied separately. Consequently, it has not been possible to establish cross-correlations between various types of electromagnetic fields through standard signal-processing techniques.

"To remedy this situation, this paper describes the application of MESA (a previously described computerized, multi-energy sensor array for the detection and recording of low frequency energy fluctuations) for researching the electromagnetic properties of hauntings, poltergeist-like episodes and other anomalous phenomena."

Another quite amazing academic paper titled ***A Responsive Poltergeist: A Case from South Wales***, by David Fontana was published in 1991.

A synopsis of his paper states: *"A stone-throwing poltergeist in an engineering workshop is investigated over a period of several months. The disturbances include small stones, coins or bolts impacting on the floor and walls;*

and reports of coins and other objects from other parts of the premises; movements of objects; large stones crashing on the roof; stones thrown at the windows; carburetor floats embedded in the ceiling of the occupants' homes; a persistent smell of burning; frequent unidentified telephone calls to the occupants' homes; planks of wood thrown violently into the workshop; throwing of stones in front of customers in the retail shop.

"A stone thrown in anger towards the focus of the disturbance is returned and the process repeated several times. A request to bring a pen results in a pen appearing in a space where it was not seen previously.

"The investigator observes some of the incidents, notably the reciprocal stone-throwing, which he finds he can reproduce on separate occasions. The phenomena end temporarily when one of the occupants leaves and the premises are refurbished.

"The possibility of fraud is discussed in detail, but motives and opportunities are found to be scarce and the occupants show themselves over a period to be reliable and sincere. Unusually, no children or adolescents are involved and the family seems stable."

Former paranormal sceptic Richard Sugg, a lecturer in Renaissance Literature at Durham University, has devoted much of his recent studies into ghosts and the paranormal. He is the author of a number of books including ***The Smoke of the Soul*** (2013) and ***A Century of Supernatural Stories*** (2015).

In the latter book he writes: *"Do ghosts exist? If you had asked me a couple of years ago I would have said no. I assumed at first that poltergeist incidents were the product of human trauma: the unconscious release of pent-up negative energies of one individual, usually aged between around eight and 25, and often clearly seen to be followed by the phenomena, from room to room or house to house.*

"But as time went on the ghost cases got harder to ignore. Most of these featured some degree of poltergeist activity (objects moved or hurled about; untraceable noises; strange lights, and much more) and a surprising number were related to me privately by a wide range of people, some of whom were convinced atheists and many of whom had told the story to very few others beside myself.

"So what does historical research tell us about ghosts? It implies that they can haunt a location, rather than a person, as with certain poltergeists. It also suggests that ghosts can manifest themselves on different levels.

"Just a few days ago, stood at the bar in a noisy London pub, I had a friend relate how he was woken one night by the overwhelming sense that someone was in his room.

"The only way he could describe it, he said, was that, although he could not see anything, he felt the figure thrust its face, suddenly, to within two inches of his own. In the morning when he described his experience to the mother of the house she was quite taken aback.

"Unbeknownst to my friend, the woman's six-year old daughter had surfaced for breakfast an hour earlier saying she had seen the figure of an old man outside her first-floor window the same night. Having no idea what ghosts were, she was not at all frightened.

"Sometimes spirits manifest in successive stages (noises; vague shape; clear image of a person), and sometimes they are heard by one person and seen by another. As with my friend's experience, the person who sees it is often a child.

"In Hampstead in the 1880s a woman rented a house in which 'steps pattered up and down stairs in the dead of night; while doors, previously locked, unaccountably flew open', and where, 'often there was a feeling, even in the broad daylight, that one was being watched … by invisible eyes, touched by invisible fingers'.

"One November afternoon manifestations grew especially strong as the mother, trying to ignore them, sat reading **The Snow Queen** to her little daughter. Finally unable to bear the sound of footsteps and door handles turning, the woman made an excuse and went into the next room. She found it empty.

"But, just as she was turning back to **The Snow Queen** and the fire, the child ran towards her. "Why mamma", she said, pointing to a windowseat on which the stream of lamplight fell brightest, "Who is that pretty lady?"

"In more recent years we hear cases of police officers fleeing from poltergeist-infested houses, as Sergeant Brian Hyams admits of his experience at the Enfield hauntings in the 1970s.

"In the same decade, we have the veteran broadcaster, James Alexander Gordon, who woke one night in the notoriously haunted Langham Hotel building in London to see a strange light which presently took the shape of a man in evening dress.

Terrified by the apparition's piercing eyes, Gordon hurled a boot at it (and indeed through it) before racing downstairs to the commissionaire. Later, several other BBC employees who had used the room admitted to seeing or hearing the ghost.

"Much later still, several England cricketers and their wives or girlfriends were quite badly spooked when staying at the Langham in summer 2014. Waking around 1.30am to find his taps repeatedly turning on and off, and with the sense of a presence in the room, Stuart Broad learned that Matt Prior was wide awake and equally unnerved, and ended up sharing Prior's twin room for the night.

"Yet for many people nowadays, talking about ghost experiences is arguably more terrifying than having them. Fear of ridicule is often greater than fear of the supernatural. If you do start asking, you may be surprised what you hear – and often from people you thought you knew very well indeed," he adds.

Dr Richard Sugg

Alison Wynne-Ryder, a famed psychic medium, says: *"Although most people you ask would say old properties – or buildings that house many people, such as prisons, hospitals and castles – the reality is that any property can be haunted,"* she says.

"Spirits can reside anywhere, and they don't necessarily confine themselves to one space. Although if they feel comfortable in a particular area, this will be where most of the activity is felt."

To finish, Shropshire based paranormal investigator Chris Morris told the **Shropshire Star** newspaper: *"I am an open-minded sceptic. Typically 95 per cent of the paranormal can be explained away, and with my background as a chartered surveyor I have an analytical mind.*

"But it's those five per cent of things you can't explain that keeps me hooked. I'm not preaching to anybody and I'm not saying that anything is life beyond the grave. I don't know and nobody absolutely knows. All we do know is that there is some form of energy that reacts with our equipment.

"We don't know if it's the deceased, which most people believe it is, but the truth is we don't know, and that's what we are trying to find out. One day we are going to get a definitive answer. Science hasn't disproved any of this. We know something is happening but we don't know exactly what."

Sceptic, believer or just undecided… everything you have just read is the truth.

Keep your mind wide open and don't blink!

About the Author

Bones is written and edited by Nic Outterside, and published by *Time is an Ocean Publications*. Nic is a an award-winning journalist and creative author, who over 34 years has worked across all forms of media, including radio, magazines, newspapers, books and online.

Among more than a dozen awards to his name are *North of England Daily Journalist of the Year, Scottish Daily Journalist of the Year, Scottish Weekly Journalist of the Year* and a special award for investigative journalism. In 1994, 53 MPs signed an Early Day Motion in the UK House of Commons praising Nic's research and writing. In 2016 Nic was awarded an honorary doctorate in written journalism. **Bones** is his ninth published book.

Books
Author and Editor:
The Hill - Songs and Poems of Darkness and Light
Another Hill - Songs and Poems of Love and Theft
Luminance - Words for a World Gone Wrong
Blood in the Cracks
Asian Voices
Asian Voices – the Director's Cut
Death in Grimsby – 50 Years Following Brighton & Hove Albion
Don't Look Down
Bones – the Mystery of Plympton Cottage

Bibliography

1. J.E. Auden, *'Ecclesiastical history of Shropshire during the Civil War, the Commonwealth and the Restoration', Transactions of the Shropshire Archaeological Society* (1907)
2. H.P Lovecraft, *Beyond the Wall of Sleep* (1919)
3. Alfred Watkins, *The Old Straight Track* (1925)
4. W.J. Farrow, *The Great Civil War in Shropshire* (Shrewsbury, 1926)
5. T.C. Duggan, *A History of Whitchurch, Shropshire* (1935)
6. Albert Camus, *La Peste* (novel) (1947)
7. R.F. Skinner, *Nonconformity in Shropshire 1662–1816* (Shrewsbury, 1964)
8. Reuben Merliss, *The Year of the Death (novel)* (1965)
9. C. Creighton, *A history of epidemics in Britain* (London, 1968 edition)
10. Philip Ziegler, *The Black Death* (1969)
11. P. Clark and P. Slack, *English Towns in transition 1500–1700* (Oxford, 1976)
12. P. Edwards, *'The farming economy of north-east Shropshire in the seventeenth century'* (unpublished D.Phil. thesis, University of Oxford, 1976)
13. P. Slack, *The Plague Reconsidered* (Local Population Studies, Matlock, 1977)
14. John Hatcher, *Plague, Population and the English Economy* (1977)
15. E.A. Wrigley and R.S. Schofield, *The population history of England 1541–1871: a reconstruction* (London, 1981)
16. R.S. Schofield, *'Crisis mortality', in M. Drake, ed., Population studies from parish registers* (Local Population Studies, 1982)
17. Dyer. A, *'Epidemics of measles in a seventeenth-century English town', Local Population Studies* (1984)
18. John Morris, *The Domesday Book – Shropshire* (1985)
19. *Victoria County History: Shropshire* (London, 1985)
20. Whiteman. A, ed, *The Compton Census of 1676: a critical edition* (London, 1986)
21. David Fontana, *A Responsive Poltergeist: A Case from South Wales* (1991)
22. P.M.H. Atwater, *Beyond the Light* (1994)
23. Sylvia Watts, *Some Aspects of Mortality in Three Shropshire Parishes in the mid 17th Century* (1995)
24. John Wacher, *The Towns of Roman Britain* (1997)

25. James Houran, Rense Lange, *Rationale and Application of a Multi-Energy Sensor Array in the Investigation of Haunting and Poltergeist Cases* (1998)
26. Madge Moran, *Vernacular Building of Whitchurch and Area: and Their Occupants* (1999)
27. Jim Hewitson, *Dead Weird* (2004)
28. Jean North, Madge Moran, Joan Barton, *The Old Rectory, Whitchurch* (2006)
29. John Hatcher, *The Black Death: An Intimate History* (2008)
30. Paul Anderton, *Exploring Whitchurch History – Growth of a Shropshire Town* (2009)
31. Shropshire History, *Shropshire Deserted Villages* (2012)
32. Richard Sugg, *The Smoke of the Soul* (2013)
33. Richard Sugg, A Century of Supernatural Stories (2015)
34. The Shropshire Star, *Archaeologists unearth Roman remains in Whitchurch* (16 November 2016)
35. The Independent, *Plague pit with skeletons of 48 Black Death victims, including 21 children, found at abbey in Lincolnshire* (30 November 2016)
36. Peter Gaunt, *The English Civil War* (2017)
37. The Shropshire Star, *Paranormal Investigators Capture Ghostly Goings On* (24 January 2017)
38. Pam Crabtree, *Early Medieval Britain: The Rebirth of Towns in the Post-Roman West* (2018)
39. Nina Kahn, *What Do Dreams About Ghosts Mean?* (2018)
40. *Whitchurch parish register and churchwarden's accounts* (transcript in SRRC)

Picture Credits

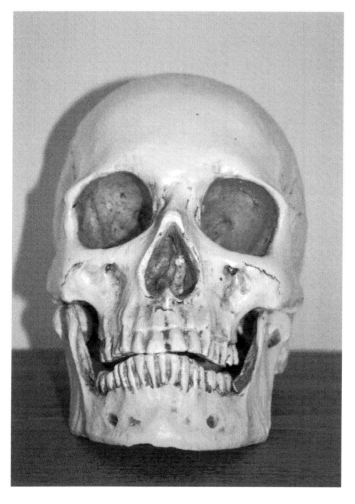

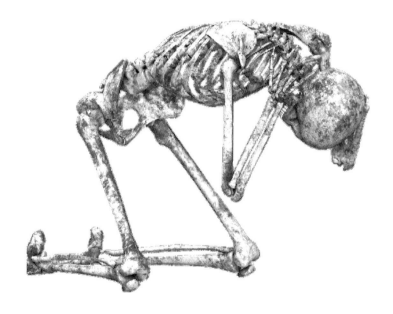

whitchurchbones@gmail.com